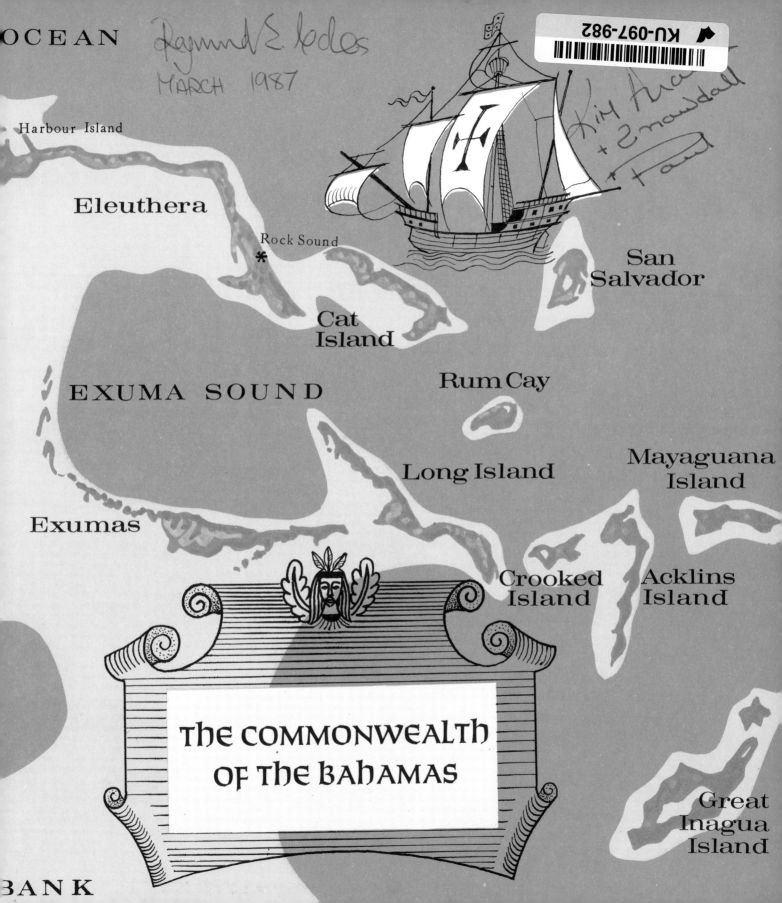

OCEAN

KU-097-982

Harbour Island

Eleuthera

Rock Sound
*

San
Salvador

Cat
Island

EXUMA SOUND

Rum Cay

Long Island

Mayaguana
Island

Exumas

Crooked
Island

Acklins
Island

THE COMMONWEALTH
OF THE BAHAMAS

Great
Inagua
Island

BANK

THE BAHAMA ISLANDS

THE COMMONWEALTH
OF THE BAHAMAS

HANS W. HANNAU

THE BAHAMA ISLANDS

WITH 86 COLOR PHOTOGRAPHS AND 14 MAPS

ARGOS INC.
MIAMI

End paper and maps by H. Felix Kraus

Published

by

ARGOS INC.

MIAMI, FLORIDA

ISBN: 0-912458-86-0

All rights reserved by Author and Publisher

PRINTED IN SPAIN

Dep. Legal B-19.641-XIII

INTRODUCTION

They are the South Sea Islands of the Atlantic, forever green and sun-kissed and forever frost-free. They have thousands of miles of perfect coral-sand beaches, many still free of footprints. The warm waters around their shores are pellucid, ranging in color from Gulf Stream blue to a dancing green that is as pretty as the leaves of spring. The climate is all but flawless. Perhaps the occasional hurricane that roars through – putting people in their place and teaching them that the ocean cannot be bulldozed – adds something that appeals to what is wild and raging in the heart of man. Fish fill the waters. Sunken treasures of gold and silver from the Incas lie waiting to be found in clear and shallow offshore depths. For at least a millennium and probably for far longer back in time, people lived largely on the bounty of the sea, as many do today. Life can be idyllic here.

The modern discovery of the Bahamas has been made by the wealthy and imaginative. They were looking, after World War II, for out-of-the-way perfection, hideaways where life has a leisurely and friendly flavor. In the Bahamas, boatmen, artists, fishermen, and millionaires found what they sought. They have shown the way to the multitudes who are following them. Along with enterprising and responsive Bahamians, this new generation of discoverers is providing the amenities needed by those who are looking for a new, kinder, and more beautiful life. The men and women who are building tomorrows in the Bahamas are not imitators. The homes, the resorts, the marinas, the architecture – the entire life they are fashioning on so many islands that were so long asleep – have a special flavor of their own. There are whiffs of a past that is as romantic as it was precarious. There is a free and easy British colonial flavor. And there is the musical rhythm of Africa.

This island empire of the Atlantic is scattered over a hundred thousand square miles. The Bahamas are sprinkled in an arc that stretches 750 miles, from fifty miles east of Palm Beach southeastward to within fifty miles of Haiti and Cuba. There are said to be seven hundred of the islands, the smaller ones usually called cays, and many more rocks and sandbars. Only twenty-two of the cays have permanent settlements. They rise from the shallows of the Little Bahama Bank and the Great Bahama Bank. Mile-deep ocean canyons cut across the banks. They offer a sea heaven for those who are exploring the ocean for fun or profit. Glamorous resort playgrounds are rising across the creek from quaint fishing villages.

The voices of the islanders have a special lilt that is all their own. There, generations of men learned to be brave when they had to and not to worry about tomorrow. There, this generation, black and white together, is working to build up the confidence and interest of the world outside, thinking of the future as well as of the exciting present. They truly believe that people live longer in the Bahamas and are interested in showing visitors how this is done.

Nassau, for a long, long time, was the sole town of any consequence in the colony. Today the enterprise, the development, the resorts, the industries, the imagination, and the people are spreading month by month to more and more of the Family Islands. The vibrant optimism strums across miles of water. Jets land at many airports. Yachtsmen are being welcomed at new marinas everywhere. Movie stars and moviemakers wander afar. Undersea adventurers have their favorite reefs, and each confides that his is the most beautiful in the world. Missile-tracking stations link the islands to the space age. It is a land that offers opportunities for all — those who want to get away from it all and those who want to pioneer on a new frontier.

The Old Government House (old print)

6

HISTORY

Will men find in the Bahama waters the first conclusive evidence of the lost Atlantis? There is some evidence that the islands have had an ancient culture receding back into the remote past. In any event, the first known European to step ashore in the Bahamas found no Atlantis. On a benign and moonlit autumn night, October 12, 1492, an adventurous Italian sighted one of the Bahama Islands and discovered a new world—by mistake. Like many men before him, Christopher Columbus of Genoa thought the world was round. Unlike competent astronomers of ancient Greece and his own time, who had a rather accurate notion of the size of the earth, he thought it was about one sixth the size it really is. Through this flaw in his calculations he was able to enlist the support of their Spanish majesties, King Ferdinand and Queen Isabella, in his project of finding a quicker route to the wealth of the Indies by sailing west rather than by going eastward. To Rodrigo de Triaña, the forecastle lookout on the smallest ship in Columbus's fleet, the caravel *Pinta*, goes the honor of crying, "Tierra! Tierra!" when he sighted a silver strand of beach in the moonlight.

The gentle native Indians, Lucayans, who fled before the Spaniards when they landed, called the island Guanahani. Columbus called it San Salvador. Later it was named Watling's Island, for a disreputable buccaneer. It has been rechristened San Salvador, and it is now officially decreed that America's discoverer first stepped foot on the New World at this place.

He found a race of fifteenth-century "flower children." Columbus described the Lucayans thus: "All of them go about naked, even the women, although I saw but one girl, all the rest being young men, none of them being over thirty years of age; their forms are well proportioned, their bodies graceful and their features handsome. Their hair is as coarse as the hair of a horse's tail and short. They wear their hair over their eyebrows, except a little hank behind, which they wear long and never cut. Some of them paint themselves black (they are of the color of the Canary Islanders, neither black nor white), some paint themselves white; some red, and some with whatever they find; some paint their faces, some their whole body, some their eyes only; and some their noses only."

Lucayan women had a reputation for being very beautiful. It was also reported that the islanders had more civilized morals than those who lived farther from "the cultivated regions of Bimini and Florida." The Indians sang and danced and were generous to the Spaniards. The sailors who landed found the Lucayans growing cotton and weaving cloth, and sleeping in what they called "hammocks" made from the cloth. Within the next ten years the sailors of many of the navies of Europe, who had been sleeping on deck and in the bilge with roaches, were sleeping in hammocks, perhaps the Lucayans' greatest gift to Europe. The Lucayans also gave the English language other words describing products of their world: avocado, barbecue, buccaneer, canoe, Carib, cannibal, cay, guava, hurricane, iguana, maize, manatee, pirogue, potato, and tobacco.

The Indians who called themselves Lucayans were Arawaks, and their migration pattern had been northward from the backwoods of Venezuela and the Guineas. They were fleeing before fierce Caribs, who not only enslaved them but also ate them. The cannibal Caribs believed in a heaven in which the brave would all have Arawak slaves, it is reported. The Lucayans had pottery, though they must have brought it over the water to the islands with them in the big log canoes Columbus described. There is no clay suitable for making pottery in the Bahamas. They drew crude pictures in stone, had a few gold ornaments, stone arrow points, bone fishhooks, tattoos, necklaces, and a good ball game in which villages entered competing teams. They smoked pipes and something like cigars, and made beer from maize or cassava. Their houses were framed with tree trunks and slender poles and thatched with palmetto fronds. Seminole Indians in Florida today find such roofs are usually watertight for about nine years.

The Lucayans had two supreme gods, a lady and a gentleman god. They believed in a heaven where there were no bears and no snakes and no hurricanes, and no trees fell on you. They also believed in ghosts and propitiated them. There has been speculation that that was why they were so friendly to Columbus when they came out of the woods after he landed. The Lucayans soon were all gone, enslaved by the Spaniards and taken off to the mines of Hispaniola to die.

Columbus was the first of a long line of visitors to give an ecstatic description of the beauty of the Bahama beaches and the clear, fish-filled turquoise water surrounding the islands. From San Salvador he sailed to another Bahama island, which he christened Santa Maria de la Concepción and which is now known as Rum Cay. His next landfall was Long Island, which he called Fernandina. Through the channels and straits of that green archipelago he cruised, looking for the golden palaces of Cathay. He did find some five-foot-long dragons (iguanas) and magnificent flocks of birds. He wended southward to Cuba after fifteen days among the Bahama Islands that he described as so beautiful.

Blessed as the islands were in their lush green growth and warm blue seas, they did not have a great deal of fertile soil and were without gold or aught else to induce the Spaniards to stay there. No Europeans ever settled on the islands until these became important as bastions to the nations wrangling over possession of other lands in the New World. The Spaniards are reported to have taken 40,000 natives of the Bahamas to mine gold in Hispaniola and to dive in the pearl fisheries of Trinidad, for they were splendid swimmers and divers. The islands were depopulated.

After Columbus, the next man of distinction to visit the Bahamas was Juan Ponce de León, in search of "Bimini" and the fabled Fountain of Youth. His expedition landed at Mayaguana, Samana Cay, Rum Cay, and San Salvador. They sighted Elbow Cay as they sailed west. Thereafter they discovered the Gulf Stream and were amazed by this northward-flowing current that swept them up along the coast of Florida. When they landed in that region at Easter time, when it is fragrant with the blooms of palmettos and flowers, they found native Indians far less peaceable than the Lucayans. For three balmy spring months they cruised along the Florida coast without discovering anything of much consequence except the continent of North America, and then they sailed back by way of the western edge of the Little Bahama Bank. This voyage possibly gave the Bahama Is-

lands their name. F. de Herrera, Ponce de León's historian, described the water around the islands as *bajamar*, the Spanish word for shallow water, and shallow indeed is that passage.

The Spaniards apparently made no attempts to colonize the Bahamas, though there were once rumored to be Spanish ruins on Cat Island. For a while the land was referred to as being destitute of inhabitants. The first map of the New World, drawn by Juan de la Cosa in 1500, sketches vaguely some islands north of Cuba and Hispaniola: Ymey (Exuma), Mamana (Rum Cay), Samana (Long Island), Yucayo (Caicos), Someto (Crooked Island), Habacoa (Abaco), and Guanahani (San Salvador). The islands are but blobs on Peter Martyr's map of 1511. Twelve are listed in the Turin map of 1523. Throughout the sixteenth century, Spanish navigators going home from Cuba feared the Bahama banks because of rocks and shoals. Seventeen ships of a Spanish fleet were wrecked off Abaco in 1595.

John Cabot in 1497, John Rut in 1527, and John Hawkins between 1563 and 1568 were probably familiar with Bahama waters, for they were among the first Englishmen to explore and trade in the West Indies. Hawkins introduced the African slave trade to the Spanish colonies of the Caribbean. English colonists in 1585 sailed through the Bahamas under the command of Sir Richard Grenville for Virginia, via Cat Island and Eleuthera and through the Providence Channel to the Florida Strait.

England laid formal claim to the Bahamas in 1629 when Charles I granted his attorney-general, Sir Robert Heath, proprietary rights over the Bahamas and those portions of the American mainland that came to be called Carolina. The proprietor and his heirs and assignees held the land as the king's tenants and had subtenants under them, according to the terms of such grants. Their rights included the right to all whales and sturgeons, gold, silver, jewels, and precious stones and the right to build forts and confer titles. They were the law. Heath never established a colony, for he fled to France when his king was beheaded, and died there. The area was regranted in 1663 and 1670 after the restoration of Charles II in 1660. These grants led to a century of litigation, which did not concern the Bahamas, for no one was living there. The French tried to settle on Abaco Island, which they called Lucayonèque, in 1625, but their effort to colonize failed.

Like the settlers of New England, the first English settlers of the Bahamas were Puritans. They came from Bermuda after trouble had broken out between the Anglican Establishment and the minority of Independent Puritans. The pugnacious Puritans claimed they were persecuted. William Sayle, a seaman, was the competent leader of a group that he called the "Company of Eleutherian Adventurers." He had been named Governor of Bermuda three times in the 1640s, but in 1647 he went to London to solicit aid in founding a colony where the Puritans could enjoy religious freedom. The posters that he pinned up and passed around in London were entitled "A Broadside Advertising Eleutheria and the Bahama Islands" and upheld religious toleration and republicanism. "Eleutheria" was the Greek word for "freedom."

Sayle set forth with some seventy colonists in the six-ton ship *William* and landed at Governor's Harbour, on the island that was previously called Cigateo or Segatto, in the summer of 1648. He renamed it Eleuthera. There, after a safe landing, the ship went ashore and was wrecked and all stores were lost. The colonists could not have lived had their fellow Puritans in New England not sent them a vessel loaded with corn and other supplies in response to their plea for aid. Royalists in Bermuda sent about sixty more Puritans to the Bahamas in 1649, though Charles I had been beheaded in London in January of that year. The Adventurers repaid the help of the people of Massachusetts by sending a cargo of ten tons of braziletto wood (a valued dyewood) to Boston in 1650. They asked that it be sold, the cost of the supplies that had been sent to them repaid, and the remainder given to Harvard College. That sum was the largest gift the college had received since it had been founded by John Harvard's initial gift of 800 pounds.

The settlers eked out a hard existence by living on exports of braziletto and ambergris, plus salvage from wrecks nearby, such as a Spanish treasure ship cast ashore on Abaco island in 1657. By that time many of the original settlers had returned to Bermuda, and the few still living on the island used a cave for worship. Whaling was also profitably pursued.

The island that was first called Sayle's Island and then renamed New Providence was settled from Bermuda around 1666. After 1663, for a time, eight proprietors, all English earls, controlled the destiny of the sunny islands under a grant made to them by Charles II. The grant included Carolina. Three ships set sail to colonize the islands in 1669. Two were wrecked off Abaco. In 1670 the Lord Proprietors of the Carolinas took over New Providence Island, where 500 settlers were growing good cotton, "gallant" tobacco, and sugar cane. The settlers petitioned the Proprietors to send them small arms and ammunition, a godly minister, and a good smith. Hugh Wentworth was appointed the first governor by the Proprietors, but he died in Barbados on his way to the islands. Captain John Wentworth, his brother, was then given the post. Though he was a popular sea captain, some settlers complained that he debauched himself and led the people to drink, causing them to go a-coasting in shallops — a lazy course of life — to the neglect of their crops.

In the first census of the Bahamas in 1671 there were 1,097 inhabitants listed. Of these, 913 lived in New Providence and 184 lived in Eleuthera Island. There were 443 slaves in the total population. The settlers were having a hard time of it. Governors were corrupt or incompetent or both.

Those were the days when the buccaneering raids of Sir Henry Morgan on the Spanish Main became legendary. After numerous raids back and forth between the Spanish and English colonies, the Spaniards seized and sacked New Providence Island in 1684. Almost all the settlers left the colony and went to Jamaica and Massachusetts.

The buccaneers were initially free souls from England, Holland, and France who settled northern Hispaniola, where they hunted down the wild cattle of the island and dried the meat over "boucans," open fires, selling the meat, hides, and tallow to passing ships. Gradually they organized as a company, "The Brethren of the Coast," and turned to piracy, attacking Spanish ships. They terrorized the Caribbean throughout the seventeenth and well into the eighteenth century and captured Jamaica in 1655. Port Royal became headquarters for the buccaneers for twenty years, until it was destroyed by an earthquake in 1692. When war broke out between England and France in 1689, the English pirates betook themselves to the Bahamas, where the waters were ideal for lurking plunderers.

A few settlers drifted back from Jamaica to New Providence in the 1680s. From the beginning they were pestered by pirates. Captain John Smith led an expedition to salvage gold from the wreck of a Spanish galleon near Turks Island in 1687 and brought up twenty-six tons of bullion from the clear water to take back to London. Treasure seeking thereupon made the Bahamas a mecca for adventurers of another type. Governor Cadwallader Jones, an unprincipled ruffian, "highly caressed those Pirates that came to Providence." The citizens rebelled and put him in irons in 1692. A mob of sympathizers rescued him. Six pirates and two habitual drunks sat upon the jury that convicted his chief enemy.

A more energetic and competent governor, Nicholas Trott, was sent out by the Lord Proprietors in 1694 to make an effort to resettle New Providence. He renamed Charles Town, capital of the Bahamas and the chief settlement on New Providence Island, Nassau—one of the titles of King William III. He built Fort Nassau, defended by twenty-eight guns. Acts were passed by the General Assembly to encourage new settlement. But scandal ruined Trott, too. The pirate Henry Avery captured a large ship belonging to the Great Mogul of the Indian Ocean. The ship carried 100,000 pieces of eight and the mogul's daughter, among other treasures. The pirate sought refuge in Nassau to get provisions and water. Later, other pirates were to testify that the governor shared in the booty. He was dismissed following an inquiry in 1696. The next governor, Nicholas Webb, also collaborated with pirates and lasted for only three years. Four notorious pirates were hanged in 1699 in Nassau.

The story is one of rogues and rascality, ruin and wrecks, for years. Nassau was again sacked, by a French and Spanish force from Havana, in 1703. Again New Providence was almost deserted. When English settlers drifted back, the Spanish struck again in 1706. Among the most notorious pirates who headquartered in Nassau were Edward Teach, alias "Blackbeard," Calico Jack Rackham, Steve Bonnet, and the lady pirates—Mary Read and Anne Bonny. In spite of the romance that now encrusts their memories, they were cruel villains. The woeful honeymoon between the pirates and the islanders continued until Crown government replaced the rule of the Lord Proprietors in 1717.

The man who cleaned out the pirates and gave the Bahama Islands their motto, *Expulsis Piratis Restituta Commercia* ("The Pirates Have Been Expelled and Commerce Restored"), was Captain Woodes Rogers, the first royal governor. He was famous for a privateering voyage round the world during the War of the Spanish Succession. On that globe-encircling voyage between 1708 and 1711, he took the great Manila Galleon and many other prizes. In 1718 he was appointed captain general and governor-in-chief of the Bahama Islands by King George I.

Some Harbour Islanders greeted him with the information that there were over a thousand pirates in New Providence. Some he captured and sent to England for trial. To some he granted amnesty. Others he executed. With all this going on, the Spaniards attacked Nassau again, but were repelled. Governor Rogers saved the islands from destruction by the Spaniards and possession by pirates. He spent his fortune, more than 11,000 pounds, there. His reward was to spend some time in prison in England for debt after he returned there in 1721.

George Phenney, a man cursed with a difficult and overbearing wife, followed him as governor, and he further strengthened the government. Among his orders to the people of Eleuthera was that swearing and drunkenness were to be severely punished. Though he was competent, Governor Phenney fell out of favor because of his formidable wife, who browbeat juries and even insulted the justice on the Bench. He was dismissed and Woodes Rogers reappointed to a second commission in 1729. A hurricane and conniving men

Royal Governor Woodes Rogers. 1729 (old print)

plagued Rogers, but he was instrumental in persuading the Crown to buy out the Proprietors, who still retained their title to land in the islands. He died in Nassau in 1732, the first really honest and effective governor of the Bahamas, though one ex-pirate did call him a tyrant.

Throughout the eighteenth century the problems of the Bahamas wore down a succession of governors: Richard Fitzwilliam, John Tinker, William Shirley, and Thomas Shirley. There were 2,303 settlers in 1741. In the entire islands there was not one mason. There were no wheeled vehicles on New Providence. War with Spain recurred and brought with it the money that flowed in from privateers' prizes, but peace in 1763 brought depression to Nassau again.

The American Revolution sent an influx of Loyalists who changed the character of the islands and trebled the population in five years during the 1780s. After Cornwallis surrendered at Yorktown, the homes of Loyalists in the new nation, the United States, were burned, their land was seized, and some were lynched. About eight thousand of these Loyalists came to the Bahamas.

During the revolution the Bahamas had been captured by Spain. After the war, a Loyalist lieutenant colonel of South Carolina, Andrew Deveaux, recruited a handful of militia and Harbour Island settlers and took Nassau by an ancient strategy. He had with him about two hundred men. The Spanish outnumbered them, but the invaders took the high ground in a brief skirmish. Then the Spanish watched boatload after boatload of troops being ferried ashore from Deveaux's ships. What they didn't see was that on the return trip the men lay flat in the bottom of the boats and were rowed back to the ship, to return again standing up as, apparently, a fresh band of troops. The frightened Spaniards surrendered in the face of the exaggerated strength of the troops and shortly afterward departed.

Southern Loyalists moved in as refugees, with their slaves and their penchant for growing cotton. They received land grants that depended on the size of their families and the number of slaves they owned. By 1787 they had planted 4,500 acres of Bahamian soil in high-quality sea island cotton in the Out Islands. Men who had lived aristocratic lives learned to be competent sailors of small boats and good fishermen. They learned to eat conch. Some returned briefly to the prosperity they had known in the Old South. Then came chenille bugs, which blighted crops, ruined planters, and ended the plantation system. It was in the period when the flood of refugees was pouring in that the first newspaper appeared in the islands, the *Bahama Gazette*, in 1784. The names of many of the Loyalist families are still very familiar in the Bahamas today.

A blight equal to the chenille bug was the arrival of John Murray, Earl of Dunmore, to serve as royal governor. He was haughty and dissolute, incompetent, unpopular, obstinate and violent in nature, and poorly educated. He built forts that never fired a shot in anger, though they exhausted the Bahamian economy then and enchant tourists today. He speculated in land. He loved Eleuthera and there built a summer house for himself and laid out Dunmore Town on Harbour Island in 1791. After breaking a stick over the head of a Harbour Islander in 1796, he was ordered to return to England.

During the War of 1812 Governor Charles Cameron received letters from two Indian chiefs in the United States saying they would raise up to twenty thousand braves to go on the warpath against the United States if the British would help them. By the time the expedition from the Bahamas was planned in 1814, the war had ended. Many of the fine old houses which grace Nassau today were built about that time.

Slaves had come to the Bahamas with the first settlers from Bermuda. In 1831 there were 12,259 Negroes in the islands, and they outnumbered the whites by three to one. Of these, 2,991 were free. The vast majority had come from West Africa, north of the Congo. Many practiced Obeah, the primitive African magic, for years. Even before the decline of cotton in the islands, few plantations were very grand. Many raised several kinds of peas, yams, sweet potatoes, snap beans, cabbage, and pumpkins, as well as cotton. Hens and turkeys and bonefish were the principal meat.

After the abolition of slavery in England in 1772 it was only a matter of time before the institution would disappear throughout the British Empire. The slave trade was ended throughout the empire in 1807. In 1819 an Act was passed in England that equated slaving with piracy. The British navy released Negroes from seized slave ships, and they were freed in the islands. Free Negroes were given the right to vote in 1807. Finally, the Emancipation Act was passed by the British government and went into force on August 1, 1834. It provided compensation to be paid to the slave owners.

A transition to a period of apprenticeship came peaceably. That system, a sort of indentured labor, was finally ended in 1838. Ex-slaves had full civil rights. However, a law was passed in 1835 forbidding assemblies for "no specific and lawful object, loitering and carousing . . . in the liquor shops, loud singing or whistling, flying kites in or near highways, and calling loudly in the markets to attract customers." The maximum work that could be imposed under a contract between ex-masters and ex-slaves was forty-five hours a week, between sunrise and sunset, Monday through Friday. There has never been a case of lynching in the Bahamas.

Methodist missionaries pioneered in general education after 1800. In 1835 a Board of Education was created and the formation of a normal school for teachers was planned. By 1859 there were twenty-six public schools and thirty-nine teachers in the islands. A compulsory Education Act was passed in 1877 for New Providence and extended to the Out Islands in 1889. Education improved slowly until quite recent years, when the rate of improvement has accelerated. The art of political organization among the Negroes proceeded at the same snail's pace until the last two decades.

It was in 1848 that the Turks and Caicos Islands were separated from the Bahamas. The inhabitants claimed they never saw anybody from Nassau except the tax collectors who collected the salt tax. The mail boat from Nassau sailed to Grand Turk just four times a year. The islands withdrew to be governed by their own president and council under the supervision of the governor of Jamaica.

Throughout most of the history of the islands, the periods of prosperity were brief. Running the blockade in the American Civil War brought one of those interludes. It was a colorful time. A blockade of Southern ports was declared by the North in the first week of the war in 1861. Blockade running from Nassau became a lifeline of the Confederacy, for the South had to import manufactured goods and export cotton to survive.

Blockade running was easy and brought high profits for a while, until by the end of 1862 the Federals built special blockade ships, propellor gunboats that made running the blockade dangerous. It continued, however, because a round trip could net three hundred thousand dollars. Long, lean, shallow-draft side-wheelers ran between Nassau and Charleston or Wilmington. Belligerent ships, which to the Bahamians were Federal, were denied the use of Bahamian harbors and could not water their ships in the islands. Cotton bought in Charleston for ten cents a pound could be sold in Nassau three days later for one dollar a pound. It is estimated that some 1,650 ships made about 8,000 trips back and forth during the war. The *Robert E. Lee* ran the blockade twenty-one times, a record. It was a wild, gay period, filled with reckless chases, hairbreadth escapes. The Royal Victoria Hotel, built in 1861 as the islands' first hotel for winter visitors who were expected to come down by steamship, was thronged with blockade runners and kindred spirits, and there was a party every night.

Far was the fall of spirits and the economy in Nassau after the blockade running ended. In Bay Street thirty-four new street lights went unlit for years. An epidemic of typhus and the worst hurricane within the memory of men then living struck in 1866. Many men turned again to wrecking, an occupation that is honorable when wrecked ships and their crews are saved and cargo salvaged. It was not always thus. Nassau, which had enjoyed the gaudy days, suffered the most. The Out Islands continued to dream along. The British Admiralty at about this time began to build lighthouses along important shipping lanes to warn ships off shallows and reefs. The first accurate shipping charts were made in the 1860s.

The last half of the nineteenth century was grim among the islands. Conch shells became a valuable export for a while, and they were shipped to Italy and France for the making of cameo brooches. They declined in fashionable favor and the trade faded. Tomatoes and cigars were exported, and the Bahamas exported the best pineapples in the world. Canning factories were opened on Eleuthera in 1857 and in Nassau in 1876. Then the McKinley Tariff of 1898 blighted the pineapple trade. This economic blight was frequently assisted by the invasion of armies of rats and landcrabs. Overworked land had to be abandoned. It is still agreed, however, among pineapple fanciers that the Eleutheran Sugar Loaf pineapple is the best in the world. Sisal was planted in the 1890s, and the export of this fiber, used for making rope, mounted briefly. After the Spanish American War the world price fell.

Sponges on the Great Bahama Bank, one of the great sponge beds of the world, were found to be excellent in quality. They continued to be an important export until a microscopic fungoid killed 90 per cent of all West Atlantic sponges in 1938. With them went what had been the backbone of the islands' economy.

In the early years of the twentieth century many islanders left for Florida, where groves and farms were being planted and Miami's fantastic land and building boom of the 1920s was in the bud. Some of the islands lost as much as thirty percent of their inhabitants.

Six of the first boats bringing tourists to the islands' lovely climate and thousand miles of coral beaches were wrecked or were burnt. In 1873 about five hundred winter visitors came to Nassau. Henry Flagler, who fathered Miami's tourist industry, came to Nassau in 1898 with a steamship link to Florida and built a new hotel. He was premature.

A telegraph connection was opened between Nassau and Jupiter, Florida, in 1892, and wireless connections with Florida were operated after 1913.

In World War I almost two thousand Bahamians went overseas to fight for Britain, and most were Negroes. The French called them *soldats noirs aimables*, and they were praised by their commanding officers for their strength, courage, and cheerfulness. Doors to the world opened for them. But the war brought new hardship to the islands. The economy fell ill. The chief bank failed. There was a food shortage. Peace was welcome, though the islands' economy, such as it was, was in a ruin.

Then came Prohibition. There had been nothing like it since the days of the blockade running in the American Civil War. Rumrunning was a blessing to those people from the time the Volstead Act was passed in 1919 until Repeal in 1933. Nassau, Grand Bahama Island, and Bimini were the principal bases for the rumrunners—the latter two because they were so near the Florida coast. Small, fast boats that could outrun any U.S. Coast Guard vessel afloat took cases of whiskey, gin, rum, and even beer into the coves and inlets of Florida, with Miami as the principal receiver. Biscayne Bay waters were sometimes dangerous at night, with hijackers chasing rumrunners and shooting at them, and the Coast Guard after them both. From Miami the bootleg booze went out in automobiles with specially reinforced springs so that the load would not make a noticeable sag. It was distributed all over the United States east of the Mississippi. The days of the pirates and the buccaneers lived again. Then came repeal, and the old savage Depression followed.

Sir Harry Oakes was the man who pioneered the millionaires' trek to the Bahamas. A goldminer who had made his millions in Canada, he was attracted by the reasonable pattern of taxation and became a resident of New Providence in 1934. The influx of the wealthy continues in a mounting tide, as they discover how good the Bahamas are for them and their money.

World War II was neither the blessing nor the blight that previous wars had been. Former King Edward, Duke of Windsor, arrived as governor in 1940 and served until 1945. Rich refugees from Europe swarmed to Nassau. Two U.S. Air Force bases were built on New Providence during the war. The Bahamas became strategically important during the German submarine forays in the Caribbean and on the Atlantic coast of the United States.

The war left the Bahamas with a bequest of two excellent airports and a rising tide of tourists. Since then investors have been attracted by the excellent financial climate. Condominiums and time-sharing apartments and town houses rake the skies in Nassau and Freeport. The Family Islands are joining in the exciting developments of the tourist industry.

One of the all-time historic days in the Bahamas was January 7, 1964, when the islands attained internal self-government through the adoption of a new constitution. This constitution provides for a legislature consisting of a senate and a house of assembly, and for the establishment of a cabinet, comprising the premier and other ministers, collectively responsible to the legislature. (The Bahamas still had the status of a British colony.) This was the first major change in a system started in 1728. The steps toward constitutional reform were first taken in 1956, when the growing strength of the Progressive Liberal Party in relation to the long-dominant United Bahamian Party made the two-party system a reality in the islands.

A new era came to the Bahamas when the Honorable Lynden O. Pindling, long the leader of the Progressive Liberal Party in the house of assembly, became, on January 10, 1967, the first Negro premier of the islands when his party achieved a majority of the seats in the assembly. Born in Nassau, he is a London-educated lawyer. Since assuming the post of chief executive, he has addressed himself diligently and with excellent success to preserving the growing economic prosperity of the Bahamas while attaining a higher and more equitable share of that prosperity for all the people. His policies have proved both progressive and stabilizing.

For newer developments see "GOVERNMENT" on page 106.

Peaceful Fort Charlotte, Nassau (old print)

GENERAL DESCRIPTION

The number of islands in the Bahamas depends on how you define an island. Some say seven hundred, some three thousand. Many are small cays (the Lucayan word for island) and rocks, windswept and lonely. The archipelago lies between latitudes 20°50′ N. and 27°25′ N. and between longitudes 72°37′ W. and 80°32′ W. Geographically, some of the group are the southernmost islands in the chain, the Turks and the Caicos Islands, but are constitutionally separate. The total land area of the major islands is estimated at more than five thousand square miles. Most of the population lives on fewer than a score of the major islands.

The climate is as nearly perfect as nature allows anywhere in the world. Straddling the Tropic of Caner, the islands are warmed by the Gulf Stream in the winter so that they do not know frost and have an average winter temperature of 72 degrees. The trade winds are cool in the summer, when the average temperature is 85 degrees. May and June, September and October are the principal rainy seasons. The annual rainfall ranges between thirty and sixty inches. Occasionally a hurricane sweeps through in the summer or fall, although only two destructive hurricanes have affected the more populated islands in the past forty years.

The population is growing rapidly. The total population of the Bahama Islands on the date of the 1980 census was 223,455.

ISLAND-BY-ISLAND POPULATION

Resident Population	Population Census 1980
New Providence (Nassau)	135,437
Grand Bahama	33,102
Abaco	7,324
Acklins	616
Andros	8,397
Berry Islands	509
Bimini	1,432
Cat Island	2,143
Crooked Island	517
Eleuthera	8,326
Exuma and Cays	3,672
Harbour Island and Spanish Wells	2,274
Inagua	939
Long Cay	33
Long Island	3,358
Mayaguana	476
Ragged Island	146
San Salvador and Rum Cay	804

In area, Andros, the largest, is vast, with 2,300 square miles. Bimini, one of the liveliest, comprises only 8½ square miles.

Approximate Sizes of the Major Islands

	Dimensions	Square Miles
Abaco	105 miles x 7 miles	650
Acklins	37 miles x 4 miles	120
Andros	111 miles x 22 miles	2,300
Berry Islands		14
Bimini		8½
Cat Island	43 miles x 3 miles	150
Crooked Island	19 miles x 4 miles	70
Eleuthera	90 miles x 2 miles	200
Exuma	40 miles x 3 miles	130
Grand Bahama	73 miles x 7 miles	530
Inagua	40 miles x 14 miles	600
Long Island	64 miles x 4 miles	230
Mayaguana	26 miles x 5 miles	110
New Providence	21 miles x 7 miles	80
Rum Cay	11 miles x 5 miles	30
San Salvador	15 miles x 5 miles	60

The islands rise from waters that are shallow, for the most part, but there are three well-defined channels. The Florida or New Bahama channel between the northwestern islands and Florida is followed by the Gulf Stream. The Providence channels run northeast and northwest, and from them a depression known as the Tongue of the Ocean extends south along the east side of Andros. It is more than a mile deep in places. The Old Bahama channel runs between the Bahamas and Cuba.

The low-lying islands are rarely more than one hundred and fifty feet in elevation. They have a fossil coral foundation, but much of the rock is oolitic limestone. This stone is derived from the disintegration of coral reefs and sea shells. It is hard when exposed to the air, but soft beneath the surface, and therefore makes a fine stone for building because it can be sawed while soft into shapes of any size. The rock weathers into caves, arches, and pinnacles in many places. Though much of the land area is either rocky or mangrove swamp, some of the soil is very fertile, but thin. This fertile black soil consists of decaying vegetable material in forests and "banana holes."

Excellent large timber in abundance is found on some of the islands, especially on Andros and the Abaco Islands. This includes mahogany, lignum vitae, ironwood, and bulletwood. Extensive areas are covered with pine forests. The pine is valued both for boatbuilding and for pulpwood. Timbering is being done increasingly as roads are being built in the islands.

The produce includes tomatoes, cucumbers, tamarinds, olives, oranges, lemons, limes, citrons, pomegranates, pineapples, figs, sapodillas, bananas, soursops, melons, yams, potatoes, gourds, pepper, cassava, prickly pears, sugar cane, ginger, coffee, indigo, Guinea corn, peas, cotton, sisal, and tobacco.

In beautiful birds, the Bahamas are rich. Inagua has a flamingo rookery estimated at twenty-eight thousand birds. There are roseate spoonbills as pink as Easter-egg dye, graceful herons and egrets stalking in the shallow salt marshes. Hummingbirds are common, as are flocks of green parrots, wild geese and wild ducks. The magnificent frigate or man-o'-war bird has been encountered by pilots at eight thousand feet. Many North American migrant birds winter in the Bahamas.

The season is closed on all wild birds all year round except those that are considered game birds in the islands. These include rails or marsh hens, wood doves, Key West quail doves, ring-necked pheasants, Florida gallinule, guinea fowl, black-crowned night herons, yellow-crowned night herons, mourning doves, all wild ducks and geese except whistling ducks, bobwhite quail, chuckar partridges, Wilson's snipe, and coots. The closed season for these birds may vary by law from year to year.

The islands are poor in fauna, with few indigenous mammals other than the raccoons. On some of the islands wild horses, donkeys, cattle, and pigs are found, but they are the feral descendants of domestic animals.

NASSAU

A Mecca of the influential, the wealthy, the social, and honeymooners by the thousands is Nassau, the bright and exciting capital of the Bahamas. This island has become not only one of the great resort centers of the world but also one of the great international banking centers, the Switzerland of the Western Hemisphere. It pulses with progress today, ranging from the building of tall, modern luxury apartments and resort facilities to new schools and utilities. The new beat of political life can be felt strongly, for at last the islands as a result of the new constitution have a government that is truly of the people, by the people, and for the people. The elegant old colonial homes and the massive ancient rock forts add a unique charm to the lively capital, which is drawing nearly a million visitors annually. A string of smaller islands and cays lie off the northern shore, and among them is world-famous Paradise Island.

Captain William Sayle gave Nassau's

island its name of New Providence in gratitude for being saved from a shipwreck there. He called it New Providence to distinguish it from the island of Old Providence near Honduras. It is twenty-one miles long and seven miles at its greatest width and lies approximately in the center of the islands. It was chosen as the site of the capital because of its fine, deep, sheltered harbor and plentiful water supply. Fresh water "floats" above the underlying salt water in the porous limestone rock. The name was given the city to honor King William III, one of whose titles was Prince of Nassau. Nassau's 250th anniversary was celebrated jubilantly in 1945. Some of the elegant Georgian homes on Queen Street are almost two hundred years old. The interesting octagonal library was once the jail. Nassau's oldest hotel, the Royal Victoria, is now closed. It was built to offer hospitality to the first tourists who were to come down after steamship service was inaugurated in 1860. The steamers with vacationers never came, and when the hotel opened in 1862 it was filled with bold blockade runners who partied every night during the American Civil War. The hotel's fascinating Blockade Runners' Bar was a fine place to drink mint juleps and evoke that colorful past. The gardens of the Royal Victoria are among the finest in the islands, fragrant with flowering trees and shrubs.

The Duke and Duchess of Windsor brought the island tremendous social distinction when they came here at the time he served as Governor in 1940. A stream of wealthy refugees followed. Air bases were built by the United States, under an agreement with the British government, to combat the German submarine menace. After World War II the trek of notables continued, and Nassau's homeowners today include English nobility, American business leaders, and internationally famous movie stars.

Visitors arrive in the city either by jet at Nassau International Airport or by one of the many palatial new cruise ships that dock at Prince George Wharf. Charter flights from Europe and scheduled British Airways service from London attract many thousands of Europeans to the Bahamas.

Nassau lies on the north side of the island. The heart of the city is Rawson Square, just off Bay Street, which is the main artery of commerce and finance. Bay Street is one of the world's most sophisticated and cosmopolitan boulevards, though the "Bay Street Boys," as the merchants there are called, no longer dominate politics. In picturesque Rawson Square are the government's administrative and legislative buildings. Here the two houses of Parliament and the Supreme Court of the Bahamas sit, in bewigged British ceremony.

The square and Bay Street have the largest straw markets in the world. The native sailing ships come to the nearby docks from the Out Islands with the woven palmetto plait and the sisal fiber that is used to make the straw hats, mats, purses, shoes, and souvenirs that are the principal native industry. Visitors watch the Bahamian women weaving the hats that will tell the world they have been to Nassau when they step off the plane back in the United States, England and

Canada. The products of these deft craftsmen are exported to Bermuda and other islands.

On Bay Street, which parallels the harbor's waterfront, you can buy a voodoo curse lamp or a silk brocade gown from China. Shopping arcades along Bay Street show the latest and most elegant styles. Luxuries from all the world are purveyed. Also along Bay Street are the nightclubs and the lively grog shops that thrum with the captivating beat of goombay and Junkanoo Tunes, under the reign of native musicians and singers. In Nassau you can swing all night if you are so inclined.

Here are the banks, and Nassau has as many banks and branch banks as it has hotels. Downtown Nassau's oldest building is Vendue House, on Bay Street, where slaves were once bought and sold. It now houses an office of the Bahamas Electricity Corporation. The old Anglican cathedral is an elegant edifice, and there are a number of interesting old churches. On East Bay Street the handsome old mansions of the well-to-do look down on the blue water of the harbor.

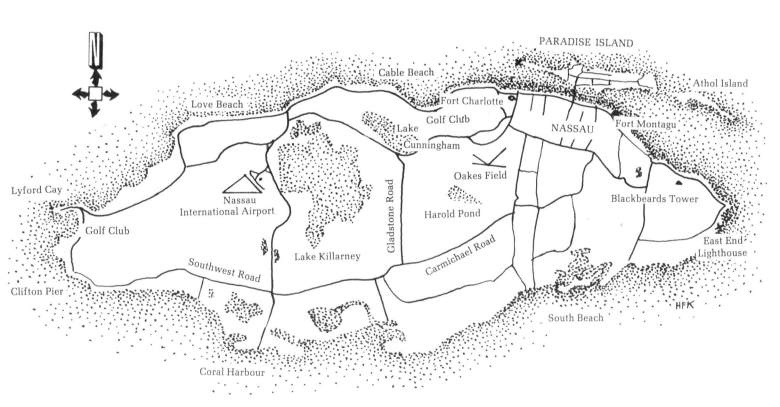

NEW PROVIDENCE

Nassau invites walking along the docks to inspect the shallow-draft native sailboats that bring fish to the fish market, vegetables, and the palm-leaf plait. They are made in the islands by expert boatbuilders and are designed for those vast shallows of the Bahama banks. They are manned by men who were born and bred to the sea and then sail them masterfully. Prince George Wharf, just off Rawson Square, is also a pleasant place to stroll about and watch the gleaming new cruise ships that make Nassau one of the favored cruising ports of call.

One of the traditional pleasures of Nassau is a tour in one of the old horse-drawn surreys with a horse that clop-clops along as the native driver spins tales and points out the sights. One of the most interesting places to visit is the elegant St. Matthew's Church on Shirley Street. It is the oldest in the colony. The graveyard is absorbing for those who like to read history on old headstones, and the singing on Sunday is something long to be remembered.

Government House, perched on one of the highest hills on the island, was built from 1801 to 1803 as the home of the royal governor, and is still the residence of the queen's personal representative in the islands. It is a handsome example of colonial architecture, guarded by ancient cannon and graced by a twelve-foot statue of Columbus. On alternate Saturdays at ten A.M., visitors enjoy watching the traditional and colorful changing of the guard.

Queen's Staircase, at the head of Elizabeth Avenue, was cut in the rock bluff by slaves. It has sixty-six steep limestone steps that mount 102 feet to the ridge. At the top is Fort Fincastle. The finest view of the island and its royal-blue water is offered from the top of the water tower on Fort Fincastle Hill. It is 230 feet high and is open to the public. From here one can see how the island is divided by Prospect Ridge, called simply "The Hill" by the townfolk of Nassau. "Over the Hill" from downtown Nassau is Grant's Town, where freed slaves settled after 1838 and where today the majority of Nassau's residents live, in homes shaded by lacy casuarinas, palms, and royal poincianas. Along the ridge are great mansions, many of a gracious colonial style.

All Nassau's massive old stone forts date back to the eighteenth century. The oldest is Fort Montagu, overlooking the eastern entrance to the harbor at the end of Montagu Hotel Beach. Fort Charlotte, complete with moat, was built during 1786-1798 to guard the western approaches to Nassau by Governor

(continued on page 54)

Bahama Waters, Great Bahama Bank

On Treasure Cay, Abaco

Hope Town Harbour, Abaco →

← Man of War Cay, Abaco

Entrance International Bazaar, Freeport

GRAND BAHAMA

Bahamas Princess Golf Club, Freeport/Bahamia

29

Underwater Discovery: Treasure of Lucaya Grand Bahama

Fishing is excellent around Grand Bahama

GRAND BAHAMA

Beach and Tennis Courts, Holiday Inn Freeport/Lucaya

The Casino Building

EL CASINO
FREEPORT, GRAND BAHAMA

The Gambling Room

31

Straw Market, Freeport, Grand Bahama

Hotel Beach at Freeport/Lucaya, Grand Bahama →

Native Musician, Grand Bahama

*One of several waterfalls
in the Garden of the Groves*

*Garden of the Groves,
a showplace of Grand Bahama
in Freeport-Lucaya*

*Subtropical Forest
in the Garden
of the Groves*

35

*Unique swimming
pool of the
Bahamas Princess
Hotel, Freeport*

GRAND BAHAMA

*The Magnificent White Sand
Beaches on the Southern Shores
of Grand Bahama*

*Service Clubs
of Freeport*

*Lucayan
Country Club
Freeport/Lucaya*

GRAND BAHAMA

*Evening Service
at the
Anglican Church
Freeport*

Cape Eleuthera Marina

ELEUTHERA

Cupia Cay,
Central Eleuthera

Cotton Bay Club
and Golf Course,
Southern Eleuthera

39

Alice Town, Eleuthera

*The Glass Window,
Narrowest Point
of Eleuthera*

⟶

Harbour Island

40

————————→

Beach Idyll, Eleuthera

Spanish Wells

The Village of United Estates

Endless White Sand Beaches

On Historic San Salvador

Riding Rock Inn

*. . . Where Columbus
First Landed
in the
New World*

*On Historic
San Salvador*

Dixon Hill Lighthouse

Mexican Olympic Games Memorial (1968)

Sea Garden Idyll

Coral Grotta with Seafans and Gorgonians

Pink Plumeworms

*In the Clear, Warm
Waters of the Bahamas*

Seafans and Grunt

46

Pink Poui Tree

Yellow Elder, National Flower of Bahamas

Royal Poinciana

FLOWERS OF THE BAHAMAS

Chinese Hibiscus

Sky Vine

Bougainvillaea

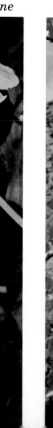

page 25

BAHAMA WATERS

The green color of the clear, shallow waters, with nuances varying to yellow and blue, is typical of the Bahama Bank. Shadows of clouds on the sea bottom dance in the foreground, in vivid contrast to the brilliant reflections of the white clouds in the background. The picture was taken in the northern part of the Great Bahama Bank. There the water is shallow: bajamar *in Spanish, from which in the sixteenth century came the name Bahama.*

page 26

ON TREASURE CAY, ABACO

One of the many cays of Great Abaco is Treasure Cay, with beautiful sandy beaches on the leeward side. The promising development here includes the Treasure Cay Yacht and Country Club and a marina with dockage for forty yachts.

page 27

HOPE TOWN HARBOUR, ABACO

The candy-striped lighthouse at Hope Town Harbour on Elbow Cay is one of the landmarks of the Bahamas. It is a safe hurricane haven, and the quaint town offers good accommodations.

page 28

MAN OF WAR CAY AND HARBOUR, ABACO

Shipbuilding is the main industry here, and it keeps everybody busy. The little island, rich in scenic beauty, is blessed with fine beaches and fertile soil, in which citrus and vegetables flourish. The harbor is one of the safest in the Bahamas. The people of the island are famous for their hospitality and friendliness.

page 29

ENTRANCE TO INTERNATIONAL BAZAAR, FREEPORT, GRAND BAHAMA

The picture shows the entrance to one of the great attractions of Freeport, a multimillion-dollar showplace of shops and restaurants with sections typical of Scandinavia, France, Arabia, China, Germany, Spain, Japan, India and England. The surroundings of the streets, squares, shops, and cafés are authentic.

page 29

BAHAMAS PRINCESS GOLF CLUB, FREEPORT, GRAND BAHAMA

Freeport is a golfer's paradise. Here you may play 126 holes of golf without

←

Tropical Flowers all over the Bahamas

repeating one hole, on fairways that are forever green. The picture shows the Bahamas Princess golf course with the clubhouse in the background.

page 30

FISHING IS GREAT IN THE BAHAMAS

With fish in abundance — sailfish, marlin, tuna, wahoo, kingfish, barracuda, dolphin, amberjack, grouper, bonefish, and many more — the Bahamas are a paradise for fishermen. The picture was taken at West End, Grand Bahama.

page 30

THE TREASURE OF LUCAYA, GRAND BAHAMA

The photograph shows a small part of a Spanish treasure of the seventeenth century. It was found in 1965 in twenty feet of clear water in front of the Lucayan Beach Hotel. Gary Simmons, water skiing and diving instructor at the hotel, noticed an ancient anchor there, dived for it, and found thousands of silver coins bearing the insignia of Philip the Fourth of Spain. The treasure is valued at about two million dollars. Experts believe there are at least three more treasure sites in the waters just off Grand Bahama.

page 30

BEACH AND TENNIS COURTS, HOLIDAY INN, LUCAYA

This picture, taken from the Atlantik Beach Hotel overlooking an excellent tennis court, the gardens and beach of Holiday Inn, shows the closeness of sports facilities in Lucaya. People living there find it easy to enjoy a variety of sports.

page 31

EL CASINO, FREEPORT, GRAND BAHAMA

El Casino stands in a park with elegant planting, in the heart of downtown Freeport. Built in the style of a Moorish palace, it has one of the largest gaming rooms, an excellent restaurant, El Morocco, and a night club, The Kasbah, with outstanding international shows.

page 32

STRAW MARKET, FREEPORT, GRAND BAHAMA

Straw markets are found on most of the larger Bahama Islands, but the most colorful are those of Freeport and Nassau. The picture shows a typical sales array of baskets, hats, and other practical items. They are made in homes and are also brought from other islands, principally northern Eleuthera and Abaco, to the markets of Freeport and Nassau.

CUPID CAY AT GOVERNORS HARBOUR, ELEUTHERA

This is the oldest white settlement in the Bahamas. It is the historic village where the Eleutherian Adventurers landed and first settled in 1649. Many quaint old houses are found here.

CAPE ELEUTHERA MARINA

Cape Eleuthera is the largest and most developed resort on the island of Eleuthera. There are elegant yacht and country club facilities with restaurants, guest villas set apart from residential villas and townhouses, a big swimming pool, the 18-hole championship golf course and the unique marina with 26 docking slips and a 400 ft. commercial dock, accommodating vessels up to 200 feet. Channel depth is 14 ft.

There is excellent fishing all along the beach and the dropoff to the South, producing Marlin, Sailfish, Tuna, Bonito, Wahoo and Dolphin.

COTTON BAY CLUB AND GOLF COURSE, ELEUTHERA

One of the outstanding golf courses in the Bahamas, this championship eighteen-hole course directly on the Atlantic ocean was designed by Robert Trent Jones. The pictures show also the Cotton Bay Club with its beautiful white sand beach and the cottages directly on the Atlantic Ocean.

ALICE TOWN, ELEUTHERA

The picturesque village of Alice Town sits on a peninsula separating Hatchet Bay from the open sound. The picture shows the sound in the foreground just behind the village, Hatchet Bay, and the coast of the island. Hatchet Bay is one of the most splendid landlocked harbors in the Bahamas and one of the safest havens in a hurricane.

THE GLASS WINDOW, NARROWEST POINT OF ELEUTHERA

This wild, romantic rock formation separates the Atlantic Ocean, to the right, from the sound, visible under the bridge and extending to the west of Eleuthera.

HARBOUR ISLAND

Just off the northern coast of Eleuthera is Harbour Island, with Dunmore Town as its principal settlement. In 1880 it was the second most important town in the Bahamas and had three sugar mills and a thriving shipyard. It is a mecca for bonefishermen and has several excellent hotels and fine beaches, which make it one of the most popular resorts of the Out Islands.

SPANISH WELLS, ELEUTHERA

This quaint old fishing town on St. George's Cay near the northwestern shore of Eleuthera is inhabited by descendants of Eleutherian Adventurers and Loyalists, and its population is about one hundred percent white. Famous for its excellent drinking water, the town got its name from the Spanish ships that often stopped there to take on water in this good harbor.

page 43
BEACH IDYLL, ELEUTHERA
For approximately sixty miles Eleuthera has excellent white-sand beaches, principally on the Atlantic. There are also a few tawny-sandy shores on the western coast. The sand dunes offer beautiful hideaways, such as this one near Rock Sound.

page 44
ON SAN SALVADOR
Upon this island Columbus landed on October 12, 1492, setting foot for the first time in the New World. The upper picture shows one of the picturesque villages, named United Estates, on the northern coast, a view from Dixon Hill Lighthouse. The photograph on the lower left is a view over the beautiful beach on Bonefish Bay. Next to it is a picture of Riding Rock Inn, the little hotel on the ocean next to the airport.

page 45
ON SAN SALVADOR
The upper photograph shows the cross on the western shore of the island, marking the spot where Christopher Columbus made his first landing in the New World. Dixon Hill Lighthouse, on the northern coast, is the subject on the lower left. To the right is a photograph of the 1968 Mexican Olympic Games Memorial, on the top of which a torch was lighted from the Olympic torch.

pages 46 & 47
IN THE CLEAR, WARM WATERS OF THE BAHAMAS
The many reefs of the Bahamas offer unusual beauty of sea life and color. Look down or dive into the clear, warm waters to the coral reefs and you enter a fairy-tale world of spires and colonnades, gorges and forests, built by coral in different forms and colors, such as brain coral, staghorn coral, and star coral. Seafans and fascinating plumeworms give the underwater scenery a mysterious appearance, in which brilliant fish, spiderlike buckeyed crustaceae, octopuses, and other strange sea monsters swim, glide, and crawl. Many of the Bahama islands offer glass-bottom boat rides, snorkeling, and diving expeditions to observe the unusual reef world surrounding them.

page 48
FLOWERS OF THE BAHAMAS
The six photographs show tropical flowers growing in the Bahamas. But there are many more in many different colors: golden allamanda, red poinsettia, blue petrea, frangipani in white and pink, golden shower, bleeding heart, the deep-red chenille plant, lantana in many colors, coral vine, orange flame vine, shrimp plant, and many more.

(continued from page 24)

Dunmore, whose hobby was building unnecessary forts. It has never fired a shot in anger. There is a lovely public park surrounding this fort, and here on Haynes Oval cricket is played on summer afternoons.

The Seafloor Aquarium in Nassau gives a delightful close-up view of the strange and wonderful sea creatures of the surrounding waters, living here in clear tanks. Porpoises, graceful comedians of the sea, stage shows several times a day. One section shows the underwater world at night. It is next to beautiful Ardastra gardens, where flamingos drill elegantly and comically to the orders of a drillmaster.

Among the many exciting events that are always going on in Nassau are the sailing races in the harbor.

There are plenty of rental cars available for the sixty-mile drive around the island. Don't forget to drive on the left, for that is the way they have been doing it in Nassau since horse-and-buggy days. A drive around the island should be slow and easy, with stops for picnics, swimming on powdery beaches, and plenty of opportunity to savor and explore it all.

Heading eastward from Nassau, one spies Blackbeard's Tower. Legend says the famous pirate used it as a lookout because of the commanding view of the surrounding waters. Beyond Eastern Point the road winds and dips under shading trees past lighthouses and beside magnificent beaches. Three miles from Nassau is Fox Hill, where descendants of freed slaves celebrate Emancipation Day every August. Nearby on a high ridge is St. Augustine's Benedictine Monastery, with a cloister and a school. The monks take pleasure in showing visitors the model farm they have created and the very fine natural-history museum with its excellent collection of Bahamas flora and fauna.

New Providence's four country villages — Fox Hill, Adelaide, Carmichael, and Gambier — are little clusters of wooden houses. Gambier, once the center of a plantation, is close to a beach as beautiful as its name, Love. Alternating with the small, old villages are exclusive new residential and resort colonies, such as Coral Harbour and Lyford Cay, private retreat of high society. President John F. Kennedy and Britain's Prime Minister Harold Macmillan met here for their Bahamas conference in 1962.

Farther west is Clifton Pier, which offers deepwater docks and berths for cruise ships or oil tankers. At Coral Harbour, Bacardi rum distillers have set up a very large rum distillery on a forty-acre site in the 2,500-acre development. The road turns south past Coral Harbour and winds through pine forests. In these woodlands is the Mermaid's Pool, a natural bowl of fresh water that is reputed to be bottomless.

Nassau has for a long time been a favorite town among yachtsmen, skin divers, underwater explorers, fishermen and golfers, and it has ample facilities for all those pursuits. The golf courses were laid out by experts. The large charter-boat fleet is captained by skilled guides. Marinas are ample for the vast yachting fleet that comes here in the winter. One of the well-known pleasures of Nassau is a trip by glass-bottom boat to peer into the Sea Gardens, where the vivid fish may be admired sixty feet below in crystal-clear waters. John E. Williamson, the pioneer of underwater photography, filmed *20,000 Leagues Under the Sea* here. He even had an Underwater Post Office in the years before World War II.

The present peaceful boom is new in the old town's history and promises to go on with no end in sight. New resort facilities are going up all over the island. The tax advantages of the Bahamas are attracting vast amounts of new capital. The progressive new government has launched a crash program to build schools, under the direction of the Ministry of Education. New primary, secondary, and junior schools are going up. High-school fees for students attending Government High School have been abolished, and additional scholarships have been made available to those attending independent high schools. The capacity of the Bahamas Teachers College has been tripled and has been absorbed into the College of the Bahamas, established in 1973. Today looks bright and tomorrow brighter.

PARADISE ISLAND

The story of the slender little island across the harbor from Nassau dramatizes the changes that this era is bringing to the Bahamas. Paradise Island is a sliver of land four miles long, three-quarters of a mile wide, and 685 acres in extent. It lies just six hundred feet off the north shore of Nassau. The dense natural foliage and long expanses of powdery white sand beaches give it great natural beauty.

William Sayle bought the little island in the seventeenth century for $294 and named it Hog Island. In the 1930s the late Dr. Axel Wenner-Gren, Swedish industrialist, bought it from Mr. Lynch of the brokerage firm of Merrill Lynch, Pierce, Fenner and Smith. Here Dr. Wenner-Gren built his principal residence, and he proceeded to develop his domain leisurely and lovingly. He laid out terraced, formal gardens to re-create the timeless beauty of the Versailles gardens of King Louis IX of France.

In 1960 Huntington Hartford, the A & P grocery chain heir, paid the estate of Dr. Wenner-Gren eleven million dollars for the island and renamed it Paradise Island. He spent more than that amount in creating his version of the world's greatest resort. He completed the Versailles gardens and graced them with fine sculpture, ranging from Greek marbles to modern statues. To his paradise he brought a majestic fourteenth-century French cloister built by Augustinian monks and reassembled it stone by stone. The cloister is today the most beautiful and scenic attraction on the island and dominates the gardens, which have become internationally famous.

Mr. Hartford launched a resort community development that includes everything — first-rate underground public utilities, wide and scenic streets and roads, shipyards, and an excellent golf course. His Ocean Club is one of the most luxurious hotels on earth. He had Dick Wilson, a leading golf course architect, design the eighteen-hole Arawak golf course, acclaimed one of the top five in the Western Hemisphere. The course initially had water-supply troubles, which have now been completely overcome, and it has been renamed the Paradise Island Golf Club.

That was just the beginning. In 1966 Resorts International, Inc., bought seventy-five percent of Mr. Hartford's interest in the island, and the development was accelerated. A two-million-dollar toll bridge to Nassau was built and was opened in 1967. The splendid fifteen-million-dollar Paradise Island Hotel, with five hundred rooms, opened in 1968. The Paradise Island Casino, one of the largest and most elegant in the world, offers roulette, blackjack, dice, and chemin-de-fer. In the 850-seat variety theater adjoining the gaming rooms, top continental and American entertainers star.

Among the newer hotels is the three-hundred-room Britannia Hotel, linked directly to the casino by a unique arcade called Birdcage Walk. Gourmet restaurants allow guests to enjoy the best of French, Polynesian, Italian, and Bahamian cuisine, great steaks, and superb seafood. The ten-million-dollar resort complex was also built by Resorts International, and with the Paradise Island Hotel it offers every facility for conventions. Nearby is Loews Harbour Cove hotel, with 260 rooms, just across the bay from Nassau. Casual fun in the sun is the specialty of the new Beach Inn on the white sand of Paradise Beach and the nearby Holiday Inn. Many tennis courts, Olympic-size swimming pools, riding stables, and other outdoor, indoor, and aquatic sports facilities are all at hand. In 1982, 710 new hotel rooms were opened on Paradise Island when the Britannia built a 350-room extension, and a new hotel, the Paradise Grand, welcomed its first guests.

Hurricane Hole, a fine sheltered harbor, has an excellent marina to provide two hundred boat slips and accommodate vessels up to one hundred feet in length. For yachtsmen, it supplies all utilities, complete services, boat-repair facilities, and helicopter service.

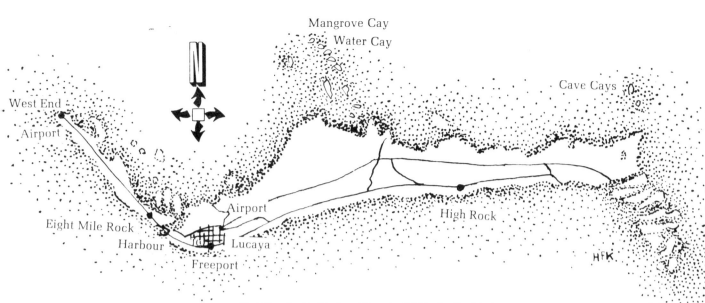

GRAND BAHAMA

One of the great jet-set playgrounds of the world today is on Grand Bahama Island. For several centuries after Ponce de León landed here in search of the Fountain of Youth, civilization passed it by and it slept in the sun. It is a rolling land with a fine stand of Caribbean pines and magnificent coral-sand beaches, but natural harbors were inadequate. No one lived on the island before 1841.

Grand Bahama, seventy-three-miles long and four to eight miles wide, is on the northern rim of the Bahamas, seventy-six miles east of Palm Beach. The rocky ridge that runs down the island is never more than fifty feet above sea level. On the south shore are some sixty miles of fine beach. In the tidal flats on the north shore, bonefish abound. Surrounding waters offer all types of fishing.

Rumrunners made the little village of West End their headquarters during Prohibition, because the island is so close to the United States. For years, ardent anglers have enjoyed the fine fishing. But there were only about four thousand inhabitants when Wallace Groves came there early in the 1950s to timber the tall pines.

Mr. Groves, an American financier-industrialist, is responsible for the creation of Freeport/Lucaya. In 1955 he reached an agreement with the representatives of the Crown and the government of the Bahamas that resulted in the Hawksbill Creek Act. Under the terms of this act, the Grand Bahama Port Authority, with Mr. Groves as president, agreed to dredge a deepwater harbor and establish an industrial area in the vicinity of Hawksbill Creek. This part of the island had large tracts of Crown lands about twenty-five miles from West End. The creek, which was navigable only by shallow-draft fishing boats at that time, bisects the island. In return, the Port Authority, a private corporation, received leases on certain Crown lands and numerous inviting tax benefits.

The agreement provides, among other things, that the Port Authority and its licensees will be free from real-property taxes, personal-property taxes, capital-gains taxes, capital-appreciation taxes, and income taxes until 1990. The Port Authority was granted the right to pass on these tax advantages to firms and individuals to whom the Authority granted licenses. Today, with the Crown land that is leased and other land purchased from private owners, the Port Authority now controls an area of 210 square miles.

A deepwater harbor was promptly built by international investor D. K. Ludwig. It has the largest oil-bunkering installation in the Western Hemisphere. Around it has been built a small and delightful world, Freeport/Lucaya. Freeport is the industrial and commercial part of the urbane little city, and Lucaya is the residential and resort portion. The numerous tax advantages have lured hundreds of millions of dollars in new investments. The community has all the modern amenities – gracious homes, excellent schools, fine resort hotels, golf courses, good medical facilities, and two gambling casinos.

Growth was accelerating rapidly. In 1963 Grand Bahama had a population of 8,230. Population in the 1980 census was 33,102, and in 1982 visitor arrivals surged to 670,620. The total investment in Freeport today is about $1 billion. Tourism is the basis of the economy of the booming microcosm, but other substantial industry includes a large cement mill, a chemical plant for manufacturing pharmaceuticals,

a soft-drink-bottling operation, and a wide variety of service industries. Freeport International Airport accommodates the largest jets, and Freeport Harbour is a mecca for cruise ships. A company owned by the Port Authority supplies electric power for much of Grand Bahama, and another such company furnishes fresh water and sanitation services.

The most important event in Freeport in 1970 was the completion of a $100 million oil refinery. The refinery is the largest unit of its kind ever built. Its base product is low-sulphur fuel oil. By-products are attracting satellite industries to Freeport. There is Burmah Oil, a trans-shipment center and storage place.

Erected here also is a tank farm with a storage capacity of one million, six hundred thousand cubic meters, sea-going pipelines that can service large tankers, and docks to provide offshore mooring facilities. The low-sulphur fuel oil helps to eliminate pollution problems now faced by public utilities in the United States. By-products of the plant are jet aviation fuel and naphtha, which is used in the manufacturing of plastics, detergents, synthetic rubber, and pharmaceuticals. The refinery employs Bahamians and is training more for technical jobs. This is the way the Port Authority is carrying out its agreement under the Hawksbill Creek Act to use its best effort to employ Bahamians and to train them for better jobs, wherever possible.

Urbane and gentle in its residential areas, luxurious and sophisticated in its resort attractions, is the garden city Lucaya. The first of the glamorous hotels and the one that launched the boom in such hotel building is the Lucayan

Beach Hotel, which opened with fanfare in 1964. The largest Holiday Inn in the world followed in 1965, and shortly thereafter came Oceanus (now Atlantik Beach), the Kings Inn and Golf Club (now Bahamas Princess Hotel), and other facilities.

A strong lure that draws a commuting stream of visitors who jet back and forth across the Gulf Stream is the continental gaming. El Casino, with an exotic golden dome that is a landmark, stands next to the International Bazaar near downtown Freeport. It is built in the style of a lavish Moorish palace and can accommodate three thousand guests without crowding.

Fine golf courses abound. Bahamas Princess Hotel has the largest golf layout in the Bahamas, with two eighteen-hole par-72 championship courses designed by the late Dick Wilson of Delray Beach. The Lucayan Country Club and the Bahama Reef Country Club have eighteen-hole courses expertly designed. Fortune Hills Golf and Country Club (18-hole course) is spectacular, rambling over 150 acres of high Lucayan terrain. Shannon Golf Club in Lucaya (18-holes) is the site of the Grand Bahama International Golf Tournament. In West End, Grand Bahama is the Grand Bahama Country Club with a challenging 18-hole, 6,800-yard, championship par-72 golf course. Additional 9 holes extend the course to 10,450 yards.

Nightlife entertainment brings famous names in show business to the island. Fire dancers, limbo experts, and voodoo artists add a fascinating variety. None of the sophisticates who trek to this new Riviera is ever bored. Nor does anyone have any complaint about the cuisine. Many fine restaurants offer a variety of delectable menus – French, Italian, Japanese, American, German, English, Polynesian, Oriental, and Bahamian.

The International Bazaar displays luxuries from all over the world and offers the atmosphere, the sights, and the sounds of five continents. It is divided into sections – Arabian, Bahamian, French, Indian, Latin, Oriental, and Scandinavian. Strolling down a Hong Kong street, drifting through Montmartre, and venturing into an authentic Copenhagen courtyard make shopping an exotic pleasure.

The basic lure is still the sun, the sea, and the sand. To those who come to be refreshed in a world that is benign to human flesh and blood, Grand Bahama offers all sorts of outdoor activities. Sailing enthusiasts can explore remote beaches by renting a speedy sailing catamaran. Water skiing with a parachute is a new thrill. There are fish for anglers of every kind of preference – except for those who favor fresh-water fishing. No license is required for any kind of angling, trolling, reef fishing, surf casting, or drift fishing. The guides are among the world's most experienced and cheerful, and charter boats are plentiful. The marinas have every facility for yachtsmen.

The clarity of the waters around Grand Bahama invites the skin diver and the undersea moviemaker. The gorgeous coral patches are so close to shore that the undersea tourist can walk out to them from the beach. The Underwater Explorers Society makes its international headquarters here. It has marine-biology and color-photograph laboratories, a research library, an underwater museum, and a luxurious sauna and gym. For novices, there are training pools and expert instructors. And for those who don't feel up to exploring the underwater world with snorkel or SCUBA equipment, there are glass-bottom boat trips to the coral reefs and patches.

The ultimate fillip was added to the underwater charms around Grand Bahama when Gary Simmons discovered a sunken treasure in about twenty feet of clear water about a thousand yards offshore near the Lucayan Beach Hotel. With three other young men who owned and operated the water-skiing and skin-diving school at the hotel, he has salvaged wealth worth two million dollars in the form of silver coins minted about 350 years ago and bearing the insignia of Philip the Fourth of Spain. He made his discovery after spotting an old coral-encrusted anchor.

With all this excitement for visitors, Lucaya and Bahamia, the garden cities adjacent to Freeport, are home town for almost twenty thousand residents. They have come here from all over the world to buy homes in a community that is designed for livability. Many are young, drawn by the pleasure of pioneering. Others are retired, making a lifetime dream come true. The architecture has a Bahamian flavor, laced with suggestions of the pastel Mediterranean style. It is not a suburban sprawl, but a model of urbane design. The commerce and industry of Freeport are only ten minutes away, but these do not infringe on the residential part of this small and lovely world.

The community has the modern conveniences – public utilities, water, churches, schools, a library, a hospital, and a Little League baseball team. Green recreation strips run between back gardens. Neighbors are cosmopolitan. There are no traffic jams.

The Colonial Research Institute has offices and laboratories at Freeport, where it operates a comprehensive and up-to-date nonprofit medical complex designed to give the growing community the best in modern medicine. There is a well-staffed hospital and adjacent diagnostic clinic.

The Institute also has other interests. It is carrying on research for an insecticide that will not be toxic to human beings. It operates a hydroponic vegetable farm. The complex includes the John Harvard Library, for which Dr. Wernher von Braun broke ground. The Institute also includes residences that are made available rent-free to outstanding scientists and physicians from leading American universities when they retire. The Institute's interests are widespread and include the financial support of nonprofit activities in the United States and other countries. The Colonial Research Institute is the creation of James H. Rand, who launched it in 1958.

Aircraft may be chartered, boats chartered, automobiles, scooters, and bicycles rented. Visitors can ride from Lucaya to Freeport in authentic London double-decker buses. There is United States-Freeport cruise service from Miami, just one hundred miles across the Gulf Stream. Daily jet flights from Miami, Fort Lauderdale or West Palm Beach, serve Freeport International Airport. Horseback riding on the beaches and riding trails is popular, and nothing rivals moonlight riding here.

Full banking services are available in Freeport at a number of banks. Legal tender is the Bahamian dollar, but United States and Canadian dollars and the British pound are readily accepted, and change is usually made in the currency that is tendered. The business community has taken steps toward building a world haven for free enterprise and international investors. There is overseas as well as local telephone service.

There has never been anything quite like the combination of government and private enterprise that has resulted in the building of Freeport. In return for the right to make more money because of the tax advantages, private investors have created a small new world. They have upped the standard of living of Bahamians and have opened educational doors for them that open onto the whole wide world. To the able, gifted, and talented who might have gone out into the world to learn and to seek their fortune, they have given ample inducement to stay at home. They have built a new Riviera for the rest and recuperation of the cosmopolitan. It is a fascinating and exciting twentieth-century pattern of action for the Bahamas, and other islands are beginning to follow this pattern, each with its own variations.

Prime Minister the Honorable Lynden O. Pindling put the government's stamp of approval on it all when he came there in 1967 to dedicate a new waterway and said, "The government is not about to kill the goose that has laid a golden egg and will continue to lay a golden egg for many years."

He went on to tell the men and women who are building Freeport, "I can see no reason why from this day forth a new and vibrant partnership cannot be forged between those of you who have visited us with your enterprising talents, because it seems to us that we can teach each other.

"We need to learn your enterprising techniques and we need to teach you how not to commit suicide, something we don't believe in. Bahamians believe in living happy, healthy lives until they end somewhere in the nineties, and they are scared to die. You like to make money, so if we can swap one or two ideas and we can learn to make some money, too, and you can learn to live until you are eighty, how much better it will be for us."

THE FAMILY ISLANDS
(The Out Islands)

The Bahamas may be defined as New Providence Island, Grand Bahama Island, and the Family Islands – which are all the rest. For several centuries the Family Islanders led a hand-to-mouth existence, and many still do. They fished and cleared their vegetable patches with cutlasses. They have always been proud and gentle people, independent and brave, with a great capacity for happiness. But their lives were very primitive. Many of the settlements sprinkled through the far-flung island chain have a history, a character, and a flavor that is quaint and highly attractive. But for ages the infrequent mail boat from Nassau was just about their only link with the world.

Today that is passing rapidly. Throughout the major islands, new resorts are being built by wealthy and imaginative investors. Airstrips and airports provide new lifelines. Radio-telephone stations are going up. Roads are being built. Real-estate developments are springing up to sell choice homesites beside magnificent beaches.

The government is bringing schools to the Family Islands, and the medical attention so sorely needed. Today there are many Family Island clinics with qualified resident nurses. Doctors have increased in number.

Brush is being cleared with modern farm machinery to plant great new farms and develop pastures that will produce the best of livestock. Farmers are learning to grade and package their produce so that it arrives at Family Island markets in top shape. Many of the larger islands are today being served by ships with refrigeration. This means that the new resorts can get frozen supplies by boat and that Family Islanders can ship their agricultural produce and fish to market in Nassau in prime condition.

Though New Providence and Grand Bahama are certainly two booming resort and business centers among the islands, other sleeping Family Island giants are awakening. Both the Family Islanders and those fortunate enough to have discovered the charms of remote hideaways are carefully preserving the quaint characteristics of old villages that date back more than a century. Serenity is the clue to the charm. Elegance is the keynote of much that is being built.

Two agencies are setting the pace of the growth. One is the group of wealthy investors who are moved to create something near their hearts' desire, after they are drawn to the islands by the physical and financial climates of the islands. The other agency at work is the government, which is determined as never before in the history of the Bahamas to bring an equitable share of the best of civilization to the Family Islands.

ELEUTHERA

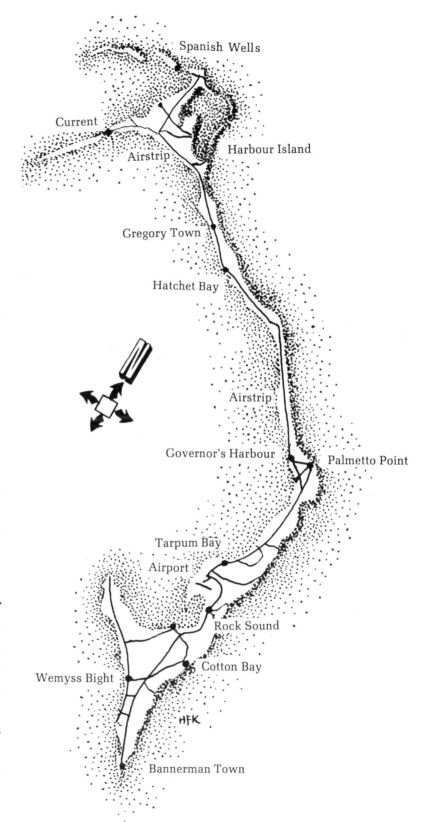

Perched on the brink of the Atlantic on the eastern rim of the Bahamas is Eleuthera, the first of the islands to be continuously inhabited. It is exotically beautiful, its rolling hills covered with subtropical greenery. There are vast pastoral green ranches and broad vegetable fields. Luxurious and exclusive new resorts have been created beside excellent harbors, with wildly romantic scenery and beaches. Ancient pastel villages cling to the shore and add charm to adjacent smaller islands on the north coast – Harbour Island, Spanish Wells, Current Island.

The island is long and narrow, and at one point the Atlantic is separated from the shallow waters of Exuma Sound on the west only by rocks. Sickle-shaped Eleuthera is 104 miles long, with an average width of two miles and an elevation of 150 feet. Seventh largest of the Bahamas, it covers two hundred square miles. Three airports offer daily flights to Nassau, New York, and Florida. Good paved roads run the length of the island. The few developers of Eleuthera's resorts are preserving the quiet atmosphere of this lovely land for those who enjoy serene luxury, free of crowds. Fine hotels and clubs and splendid golf courses and tennis courts have been built.

In southern Eleuthera the principal town is Rock Sound, picturesque and tree-shaded. Among the luxurious clubs and resorts are

Cotton Bay Club and Winding Bay. The private and exclusive Cotton Bay Club, directly on the Atlantic, has one of the finest eighteen-hole golf courses in the islands. The development of this part of the island was begun by Arthur Vining Davis of Alcoa and was continued by a group of investors headed by the late Juan Trippe, creator of Pan American Airways.

South of Rock Sound, on the southwestern tip of the island, in the Powell Point vicinity, is "Cape Eleuthera," an outstanding multimillion dollar, 5,800 acre residential resort, complete with 18-hole golf course, marina and yacht club, guest villas, condominium villas, townhouses and residential housesites.

North of Rock Sound is Tarpum Bay, a quaint old settlement favored by artists. A good road leads to the Tarpum Bay Development. Proceeding up the ridge of land, a road to the east crosses over a narrow sound to Windermere Island, with an elegant residential development, club and hotel.

In Central Eleuthera are found Ten Bay Beach, North Palmetto Point, and South Palmetto Point. Governor's Harbour, about halfway up the coast, is a fascinating, old town. Just to the north is Cupid Cay, site of the first settlement of the Eleutherian Adventurers who came here to find freedom. Fine old Bahamian homes grace the area. The town also has several excellent resorts and a Club Mediterranée. Farther north, the fine Hatchet Bay Plantations cover twenty-five hundred acres, which produce dairy and poultry products and vegetables. Nearby Gregory Town claims that it grows the finest pineapples in the world.

The "Glass Window" is a place where honeymooners should go, for it is as breathtaking as Niagara Falls. Here, at the narrowest point of the island, the ocean almost kisses the quiet Sound. A natural rock arch once bridged the rocks beneath. Washed away in a storm, it was replaced by a man-made bridge. The contrast between the deep blue of the ocean and the pale-green shoal waters of the sound is one of the most striking in all this world of beautiful water.

On the northern end of Eleuthera, where the sickle has a knob similar to the wide one at the southern end, there are two roads to travel by, and both are becoming better traveled today. To the right, going north, is Harbour Island, once the home of skilled wreckers and excellent boatbuilders and now one of the most popular of the Family Island resorts. Here are holiday homes, great bonefishing, and a parklike estate where Alan Malcolm has built a scattering of guest cottages beside a perfect beach. He calls them, appropriately, the Pink Sands. Other good resorts and hostelries are the Coral Sands Hotel, Ocean View Club, Romora Bay Club, Tingum Village, Dunmore Beach Club, Runaway Hill and Valentine's Yacht Club. There is excellent anchorage for shallow-draft vessels.

The Bluff is an old-fashioned little village with a miniature harbor. At the settlement called The Current, houses are built on low piles. Some of the inhabitants there claim descent from a tribe of North American Indians who were transported to the place after a massacre of settlers on Cape Cod. Separated from the village by a narrow strait is Current Island, where the men fish and the women and children plait nice straw work.

Spanish Wells, on the small island of St. George's Cay, is just off the northwest coast of Eleuthera. This town is unique in the Bahamas. The tow-headed, blue-eyed people are descended from the original Eleutherian Adventurers and from the Loyalists who came here after the American Revolution. They are reported to be the best fishermen and seamen in the Bahamas. The town sits on a steep hog-back ridge above an excellent harbor, with brightly gardened, red-roofed white houses crowded together. Sawyer's marina offers good yachting facilities. The people are renowned as pilots and fishing guides. Water from the wells is said to be among the purest and best in the Bahamas. There are four fine hostelries on Spanish Wells: St. George's Hotel, Sawyer's Marina, the Beach Resort and the Harbour Club.

Near the Northern end of Eleuthera is Preacher's Cave, where shipwrecked Eleutherian Adventurers sought shelter.

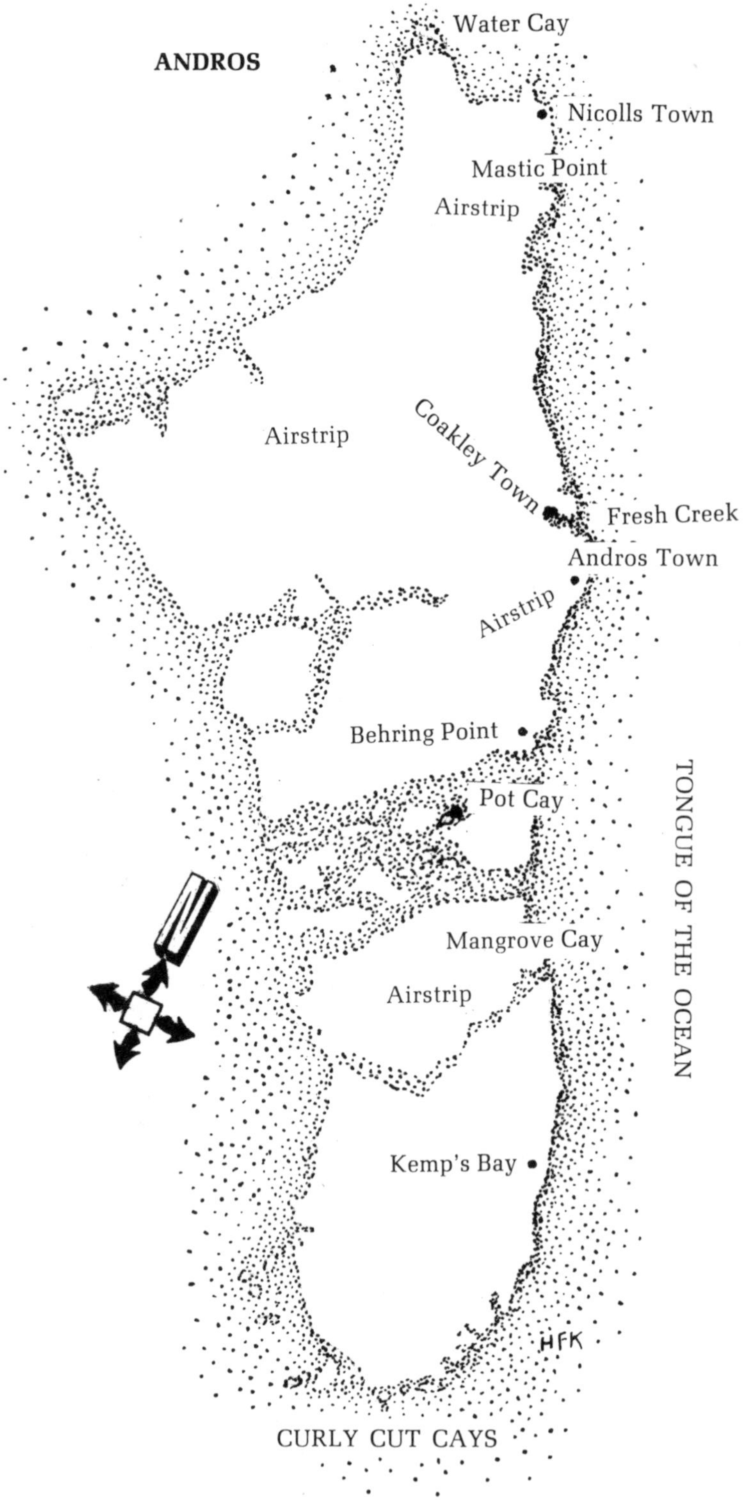

ANDROS

The giant island of Andros, one of the largest unexplored tracts of land in the Western Hemisphere and largest in the Bahamas, has long been considered mysterious. It is flat, with 2,300 square miles laced with countless interconnecting creeks and lakes. It is about 140 miles east of Miami, one of the closest of the Bahamas to Florida and one of the least known. A small native population is scattered along the shore. The inhabitants share colorful legends and the ancient art of firedancing. One of the myths is that in the interior of the island live tribes of aborigines and a lost world of long ago. Exploration by air has revealed no evidence to support this tale.

Andros is also, according to native myth, the exclusive home of the Chickcharnies, Bahamian elves that make mischief for people. They are supposed to have three fingers, three toes, fearsome red eyes, feathers, and beards. When not engaged in mischief, they are said to hang by their tails from cottonwood trees. Should a human speak against the Chickcharnie or laugh in its face, he will immediately have his head turned backward on his shoulders. The failure of Neville Chamberlain's sisal plantation at Mastic Point on Andros in 1897 was blamed by natives on the Chickcharnies.

A big impetus to development came in 1963 when Andros was chosen as the site of the Atlantic Undersea Testing and Evaluation Center (AUTEC), through an agreement between the United States and British governments. Here $120,000,000 is being spent to test

ANDROS

Water Cay

Nicolls Town

Mastic Point

Airstrip

Airstrip

Coakley Town

Fresh Creek

Andros Town

Airstrip

Behring Point

Pot Cay

Mangrove Cay

Airstrip

TONGUE OF THE OCEAN

Kemp's Bay

HFK

CURLY CUT CAYS

and track undersea devices and nuclear submarines. The site is ideal because the Tongue of the Ocean, with its thousand-fathom depths, parallels the eastern coast of Andros and is the only unfrequented ocean trench so near the coast of the United States.

The waters around Andros account for much of the current interest in the island. Just off Andros Town is a coral barrier reef that is exceeded in size only by Australia's. There is a shelf of solid sea fossils twenty thousand feet thick. It could hold oil as well as secrets of ancient times, and geologists from the Smithsonian Institution are much interested. Because Andros has never had a frost, its produce brings excellent prices when Florida freezes.

The land also enjoys plenty of fresh water.

One of the attractive resorts is San Andros Inn and Tennis Club in the Northern part of Andros. Carved out of a 7000-acre plantation originally owned by former British Prime Minister Chamberlain, it offers modern accommodations in 22 hotel rooms with a fresh-water pool, tennis and horseback riding. There are beautiful beaches and excellent fishing.

Bonefishing on Andros is world-famous, and record-breaking blue marlin are caught offshore. The resorts offer all the facilities required for boating and fishing. Skin divers find the coral reefs among the most beautiful in the world.

THE ABACOS

The red-and-white candy-striped lighthouse standing 120 feet tall beside Hope Town's deep harbor is the landmark for Great Abaco, Little Abaco, and the small green cays that surround them. This is a unique island. Fierce wild hogs, descendants of pigs brought there by buc-

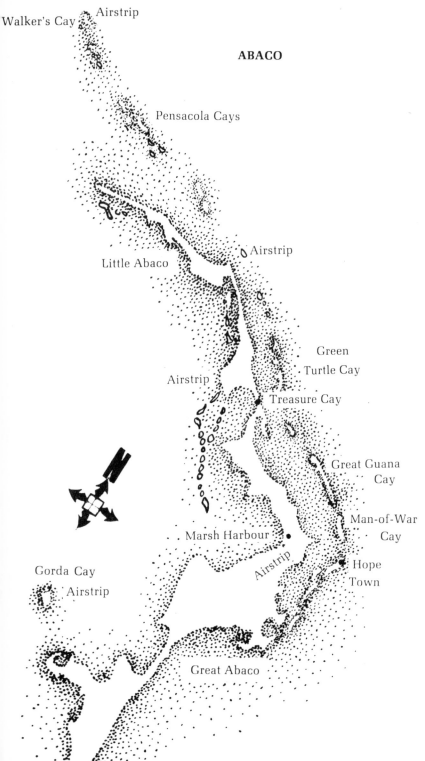

ABACO

Walker's Cay
Airstrip

Pensacola Cays

Little Abaco
Airstrip

Airstrip

Green
Turtle Cay

Treasure Cay

Great Guana
Cay

Man-of-War
Cay

Marsh Harbour

Gorda Cay
Airstrip

Airstrip

Hope
Town

Great Abaco

caneers, challenge those who make safaris into the Abaco bush. Shy wild horses may be spotted in the interior of northern Abaco. Colorful tropical parrots abound. Here also a fine new world is being built.

This island group lies 106 miles north of Nassau and 175 miles east of Palm Beach. At Treasure Cay on the east coast of Great Abaco, a beautiful resort town is being built, with five miles of beach, a power plant, water mains, fine homesites, airline service, the superb Treasure Cay Beach Hotel, a marina, and an eighteen-hole championship golf course.

Marsh Harbour is the largest town on the island and the port from which are shipped winter tomatoes and cucumbers grown nearby on six thousand acres of fertile cleared land.

Man o' War Cay, first settled by Loyalists, is the boatbuilding capital of the Bahamas. Many fine yachts and sailing vessels are here constructed of Andros planking and hardhearted Abaco pine for ribs and masts. Marsh Harbour was also a shipbuilding center but now relies mostly on tourism.

Visitors can find many attractive accommodations on this interesting island. Hope Town Harbour Lodge and Elbow Cay Club in a sleepy village that suggests Cap Cod, is excellent. Green Turtle Cay offers elegant Bluff House and the Green Turtle Yacht Club. On Great Guana Cay is the Guana Beach Resort. A twenty-thousand-dollar Spanish silver ingot was found off South Abaco in 1950.

CAT ISLAND

Bain's Town

Airstrip

Arthur's Town

Bennett's Harbour

N

Stephenson

The Cove

Knowles

Newport

Airstrip

The Bight

Old Bight

Hard Bargain Development

Port Howe

Reef Harbour Development

Airstrip

Columbus Pt.

Devil's Point

has stepped smartly into the picture in the Bahamian tourist development.

The Hawk's Nest Fishing and Yacht Club, with its three-thousand-foot airstrip and a well-equipped marina, opened in 1968. The new resort has its own private beach. The creek is filled with fighting bonefish. The club also arranges offshore angling trips and skindiving expeditions to some of the clearest waters in the world. The Bridge Inn, Cutlass Bay Yacht Club, Fernandez Bay Village, and Greenwood Inn are small resorts.

One of the most beautiful and fertile of the islands is Cat Island, with its high cliffs more than two hundred feet in elevation, and a dense natural forest. It is the sixth largest of the Bahamas, some forty-five miles long and about five miles wide, and is one of the eastern most of the islands in the chain. Hawk's Nest Creek on its southern tip is 140 miles from Nassau and 325 miles from Miami. Cat Island has one commercial and several private airstrips and a continuous road from end to end, though it does not have a deepwater, enclosed harbor. The farming and ranching that once flourished on the fertile soil has declined, but now Cat Island

SAN SALVADOR

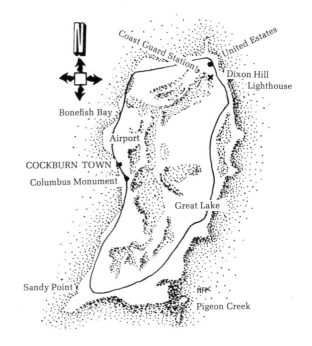

The island of San Salvador, where Columbus first stepped ashore in the New World and knelt and prayed before claiming the land for Spain, has changed little since then. It is one of the most attractive islands in the Bahamas, unspoiled, with many miles of white-sand beaches, wooded hills up to 150 feet in elevation, 28 land-locked lakes (the largest 12 miles long). There is rich vegetation, palms of several varieties, and flowering bushes along the beaches.

San Salvador has a good airstrip near Cockburn Town, on the west coast of the island, and a clean and pleasant hostelry, the Riding Rock Inn, nearby, with all modern comforts and excellent cuisine. A forty-mile shore road around the island offers beautiful views of the cays and little islands along the coast, and over some of the picturesque island lakes. Rental cars and taxis are available.

South of Cockburn Town a big cross marks the spot on the coast where Christopher Columbus made his first landing in the New World (October 12, 1492). A few steps away is the stately Olympic Games Memorial, erected in 1968 to commemorate the Games in Mexico. A Spanish ship brought the Olympic torch from Greece to San Salvador, retracing the route of Columbus. Runners with the Olympic torch circled the island and finally lighted the torch on top of the monument. A Mexican warship then brought the Olympic torch to the festivals in Mexico.

The island is surrounded by deep water.

Dixon Hill Lighthouse stands sentinel to the north, overlooking the open Atlantic and a friendly village, called United Estates, with the crumbling remains of old plantations.

San Salvador will be developed within the next decade for the coming 500th anniversary of the discovery of America. In 1982 the Bahamian government formed a National Commission to plan the quincentennial celebration. Chairman is the member of Parliament for San Salvador, Mr. Philip Smith. Channels will soon be made between ocean and lakes, opening romantic inlets for the fisherman and a passage through the island from coast to coast. There is excellent bonefishing in Pigeon Creek, lobsters up to eighteen pounds, tuna, grouper, and dolphin catches close to shore. There are plans for residential and commercial settlements, adding this lovely historic island to the more developed resorts of the Bahamas.

EXUMAS

Connoisseurs of the Out Islands have learned to love the Exumas, and knowledgeable yachtsmen have discovered that the warm waters between Nassau and the Tropic of Cancer offer beautiful cruising. There are eighty square miles of land in Great and Little Exuma, and north of the two extends a chain of countless neighboring cays and islets. Resort development is advancing. The islands are served by flights from Nassau, only thirty-five miles to the north-northwest. The government has designated a large part of this group as the Exuma Cays Land and Sea Park. The park is distinguished by being the last home of the Bahamian iguana, which has become rare since natives found that it is as delicious as chicken when baked.

Elizabeth Harbour has such a good natural harbor for ocean-going vessels that it was at one time suggested as the capital of the Bahamas. George Town is a picturesque village that becomes exciting when the Out Island Regatta is held there annually in April. Prince Philip was a fascinated spectator in 1959. There are many small hotels on Great Exuma and several yacht clubs in the neighboring cays. Americans have built numerous fine homes on Goat Cay.

Old plantation ruins dot the islands, and one old plantation house, The Cotton House on Little Exuma, still has a "squire" in residence. Stocking Island, just across the harbor from George Town, has a beach on the ocean side that is said to be the finest for shell collecting in all the islands.

LONG ISLAND

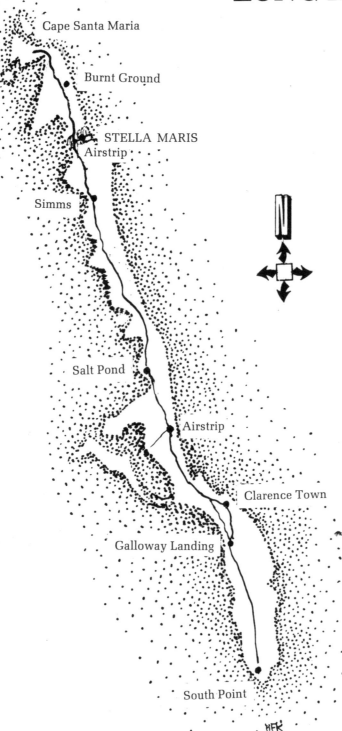

Cape Santa Maria

Burnt Ground

STELLA MARIS
Airstrip

Simms

Salt Pond

Airstrip

Clarence Town

Galloway Landing

South Point

HFK

Not far south of Cat Island is Long Island, which is well-named because it is sixty-four miles long and just over three miles wide at its widest part. In the eighteenth century, plantations thrived briefly, growing sea-island cotton, but the abolition of slavery made them unprofitable. Connected by a road that runs the length of the island are the main settlements: Burnt Ground near the northern tip, Simms, Wood Hill in the center, Clarence Town, Roses, and South Point. It is one of the few islands that had a good carriage road throughout its length more than a century ago.

Because Long Island is one of the Bahamas nearest to the coast of Cuba, it once had a comparatively dense population of Lucayan Indians who came up from the south in their long log canoes. Columbus visited the island, called Yuma by the natives, and he rechristened it Fernandina. It is rich in archeological fragments in numerous caves.

Though the plantation mansions are ruins today, Long Island is one of the chief producers of vegetables and cattle among the islands. Modern farming is replacing the machete, and Simms is an important sheep and farming center. Fertile potholes grow superior tomatoes, pumpkins, and onions, which are shipped to Nassau.

The creation of tourist attractions has reached Long Island with the building of the Cape Santa Maria Club on Calabash Bay, de-

(continued on page 102)

Oner the Central Exumas

Sunsets
Nassau

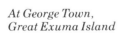

At George Town,
Great Exuma Island

Nassau: Romance and Color

The Cable Beach Hotel and Casino (Nassau), largest and newest hotel in the Bahamas (700 rooms)

One of the Beautiful Beaches of Paradise Island

View over Paradise Island

Paradise Beach, Paradise Island

← *Formal
French Gardens,
Paradise Island*

*Paradise Island Hotel
on Hartford Beach*

*Paradise Island
Golf Club*

*South Coast of Paradise
Island: Hurricane Harbor
and Loew's Harbour Cove Hotel*

*Bridge from Nassau
to Paradise Island*

Nassau the Beautiful

Government House, Nassau

Queens Staircase,
Nassau

Pirates Cove,
the Beautiful Beach of
the Holiday Inn on
Paradise Island

Gracious Living in Nassau

———→

Quiet Beach, Nassau

*Goombay Parade
on Bay Street,
Nassau*

Empress Josephine of France on Paradise Island

*Evening at
Coral Harbour,
Nassau*

86

Fresh Creek, Andros

←

ANDROS

Andros is a Paradise for Divers

Beach at Lighthouse Club, Andros

San Andros Inn and Tennis Club

Long Island: Countryside
near Clarence Town

Stella Maris,
Long Island

←

Shoals and Dunes on
the North Coast, Andros

Bimini

←

Golf Course

Cat Cay

*Secluded Beach
and homes*

Berry Islands: Great Harbour Cay

→

Flamingo Colony,
Great Inagua

OVER THE CENTRAL EXUMAS

page 73

A typical picture of Exuma Cays shows rolling hills covered with dense vegetation, and beautiful beaches. The Exumas are a string of ninety miles of cays with excellent harbors — a paradise for sailing, cruising, fishing, and diving in the wonderful water surrounding them.

AT GEORGE TOWN, GREAT EXUMA ISLAND

page 74

George Town is the only community of any size in the Exumas and is the capital. It has about six hundred inhabitants. The colorful little village is built around a public square beside Elizabeth Harbour, which offers excellent and safe anchorage. Seen in the picture is a nearby beautiful beach. Great Exuma Island is about forty miles long and seven miles wide at its greatest width.

SUNSETS IN NASSAU

page 75

All around Nassau (Providence Island) and Paradise Island sunsets can be observed, the most beautiful ones from August to October, when the air is humid and clouds reflect the brilliant colors of the sinking sun.

NASSAU: ROMANCE AND COLOR

page 76

Nassau, the capital of the Bahamas on New Providence Island, is the richest and most highly developed city in the Bahamas. Some of its quaint streets, bordered by old trees and blooming greenery, are truly romantic. From June until August the many flamboyant trees in Nassau are in bloom.

THE CABLE BEACH HOTEL AND CASINO (NASSAU)

page 77

Opened in November 1983, it is the largest and most modern tourist and convention facility in the Bahamas with a beautiful beach, 10-court tennis club, swimming pool, gambling casino and night club shows.

A BEAUTIFUL BEACH OF PARADISE ISLAND

page 77

Nassau and Paradise Island have many beautiful beaches. This one is part of Hartford Beach, one of the most magnificent ones of the Bahamas, on the north coast of Paradise Island.

FORMAL FRENCH GARDENS, PARADISE ISLAND

page 78

Connected by a bridge to Nassau is Paradise Island, a modern resort development. The picture shows the formal gardens of the Ocean Club, with the ruins of a fourteenth-century cloister, brought over from France, in the background.

←

Sunset, Cat Island

page 83

QUEENS STAIRCASE, NASSAU

Quite in the center of Nassau at the head of Elizabeth Avenue, is Queens Staircase. It was cut in the rock bluff by slaves. It has sixty-six steep limestone steps that mount 102 feet to the ridge. At the top is Fort Fincastle. One of the finest views of the island is offered from the top of the water tower, standing next to the fort.

page 83

PIRATES COVE, PARADISE ISLAND

A real romantic beach is Pirates Cove, now part of a Holiday Inn with 533 modern rooms.

page 84

GRACIOUS LIVING IN NASSAU

This spacious estate is representative of Nassau's stately and gracious style of living. There is something here of the beauty of an English estate — the wrought-iron gates, the well-groomed gardens. Southern colonial and Georgian styles of architecture prevail here. The Nassau carriage adds to the atmosphere of the past.

page 85

QUIET BEACH, NASSAU

Although Nassau is a center of tourism, there are still many lonely, beautiful, hidden beaches along the sandy coastline of New Providence Island. This picture, taken on Cable Beach, where there are many hotels, shows a spot where swimming, sunning and fishing beside the clear water can be enjoyed with complete privacy.

page 86

GOOMBAY PARADE

Folklore is quite lively in Nassau. June, July and August is Goombay Summer with Goombay Dancers parading in the streets of Nassau.

page 86

EMPRESS JOSEPHINE OF FRANCE IN THE FRENCH GARDENS OF PARADISE ISLAND

The beautiful sculpture of Empress Josephine in the nude, carved in white marble, decorates the entrance of this formal French garden. The garden was envisioned by Dr. Axel Wenner-Gren as capturing the spirit of the gardens of the period of Louis IX of France, and was completed by Huntington Hartford in its present style. It is now part of the Ocean Club.

page 87

EVENING AT CORAL HARBOUR, NASSAU

Though today the whole island is often called Nassau, after the capital of the Bahamas, it is really the island of New Providence. As evening falls, it comes romantically to life. Nassau is not all sightseeing, bargain hunting, nightlife, gambling, sports, and good eating. It is also famed for its peace and quiet, the serenity of its leisurely way of life, and the magnificent beauty of its seascapes. Coral Harbour is a serene community development, with golf course, boat slips, waterways, homes and beautiful tropical gardens beside the splendid beach.

page 88

FISHING BOATS ON FRESH CREEK, ANDROS

Fresh Creek, near Coakley Town, is on the east coast of Andros, facing the Tongue of the Ocean, with its extreme thousand-fathom depths, an ideal area for gamefishing. Nearby is the AUTEC area and just around the corner is the Lighthouse Club.

page 89

BEACH AT LIGHTHOUSE CLUB, ANDROS

There are many sandy beaches around Andros, largest of the Bahama Islands. The picture shows one of the best, at Lighthouse Club a short twenty-two-mile flight from Nassau.

page 89

SAN ANDROS INN, ANDROS

San Andros is a unique resort development carved out of a 7,000-acre plantation in northern Andros originally owned by former British Prime Minister Chamberlain. There are beautiful beaches, a mile offshore is the world's second-largest barrier reef. The fishing is excellent: marlin, sailfish, tuna, wahoo, dolphin and grouper abound. Also on "the flats" bonefishing is at its best. The hotel offers modern accommodations, with a fresh-water pool, tennis and horseback riding.

page 90

SHOALS AND DUNES ON THE NORTH COAST, ANDROS

From an airplane on the way to Nassau, northern Andros seems to be comprised of shoals, dunes, winding waterways, and swamp. The island is laced with streams and creeks, and also has numerous fresh-water lakes. Bird life is very interesting on this island, which in inland areas is covered with dense forests.

page 91

LONG ISLAND: COUNTRYSIDE NEAR CLARENCE TOWN

This is one of the leading islands when it comes to natural beauty. The soil is fertile, ideal for growing vegetables and fruit, and offering good pasture for the cattle raised here. Bananas and pineapples are major crops. The picture shows the clean countryside in the southern part, with the church of Clarence Town in the background.

page 91

STELLA MARIS, LONG ISLAND

In the northern part of Long Island is a charming new development, Stella Maris (Star of the Sea), with an airport, hotel, restaurant, marina, swimming pool, good roads, yacht dock, and many homesites. It stretches from shore to shore and has a fine beach. Developed mostly by Europeans — Germans and Scandinavians — it has the flavor of old-world charm. The picture shows a street of Stella Maris.

page 92
BIMINI

There are really two islands, North and South Bimini, close to each other. The airport is on South Bimini, but most of the hotels and resorts are on North Bimini, with Alice Town as the settlement. Bimini is world famous among sports fishermen. It is just beside the royal-blue Gulf Stream, and marlin and tuna catches are outstanding. Everything in Bimini centers on fishing — the harbor, boat slips, docks, and inns and resorts.

page 93
CAT CAY

South of Bimini is Cat Cay, owned by members of the Cat Cay Club. There are beautiful white sand beaches, an excellent golf course, a big marina, landing for seaplanes, swimming pool, clubhouse, restaurants and bars and many private homes in secluded settings.

page 94
THE BERRY ISLANDS: GREAT HARBOUR CAY

This island chain on the eastern edge of the Great Bahama Bank comprises small islands of quite different appearance. The biggest one is Great Harbour Cay, about 3800 acres in extent, with beautiful beaches and an 18-hole championship golf course. See photograph page 94. — During the reign of William IV, Williamstown was laid out on Great Stirrup Cay and a custom house was erected. — Fraser's Hog Cay and Bond's Cay, privately owned, are suitable for stock raising and agriculture. The most lively one is Chub Cay with its Chub Cay Club, Marina and Hotel and its 4,000 foot airstrip served by Bahamasair.

page 95
FLAMINGO COLONY, GREAT INAGUA

Great Inagua, second largest island in the Bahamas, is a wonderful place for nature lovers. Wild horses, donkeys, and hogs roam the interior of this big island. It is also the last retreat of the flamingoes, which once graced most of the Bahamas. In a big, shallow lake in the interior of the island, Windsor Lake, more than twenty thousand flamingoes are living and nesting. It is not easy to approach them, because they are very wary of men. However, if one moves carefully on one's stomach, it is possible to come quite close. The picture shows part of the big colony.

page 96
SUNSET IN THE BAHAMAS (CAT ISLAND)

Sunset can be a great experience in the Bahamas. Reds, golds, and greens are reflected in the clear waters. The best season for great sunsets is August and September.

(continued from page 72)

signed for the pleasure of yachtsmen. It has excellent hotel accommodations, dining and wining, and all the facilities needed by yachts. At Salt Pond is Thompson Bay Inn Apartments. The island has two airstrips.

Airlines fly from Nassau and Florida to Long Island, and have given a boost to the development of the delightful community of Stella Maris as a residential and resort area. Attractive homes fronting on white sand and blue water and backed by green hills are being built in the well-planned Stella Maris Estate. The community has a hunting and fishing preserve and an excellent golf course. The delightful Stella Maris Inn is becoming a favored resort for lovers of water sports, skin diving, and fishing, and offers hotel rooms and apartments, plus delicious dining.

The 3,400 natives of Long Island have won a reputation for being expert boat-builders and sailors by winning a large number of "firsts" in the Out Island Regatta at George Town.

RUM CAY

An island with rolling hills, golden beaches, and winter duck shooting is Rum Cay, twenty miles southwest of San Salvador. Columbus gave it quite a different name – Santa Maria de La Concepción. Its one small settlement, Port Nelson, is home to fewer than a hundred hospitable inhabitants. Loyalist planters settled this cay, and it was once famous for pineapples, stock, and salt. There are roads on the island, but horses make a refreshing substitute for automobiles. The Rum Cay Diving Club is at Port Nelson.

BERRY ISLANDS

Dear to the hearts of sailors, yachtsmen and fishermen are the Berry Islands. They include some thirty islands and almost a hundred small cays. They are on the edge of the Providence Channels, only twenty-eight miles from Nassau at the nearest point, and they offer deep-sea fishing in adjacent waters second only to Bimini. Chub Cay, at the southern end of this group, has fine yacht-club facilities. There is a private four-thousand-foot airstrip on Chub Cay, with its Marina & Hotel.

The most northern island is Great Stirrup Cay. During the reign of William IV, Williamstown was laid out on it and a Custom House was erected.

Next to the south, Great Harbour Cay is the biggest of the island group with 3,800 acres in extent. (See photo on page 94.)

A few of the smaller cays are inhabited by sponge fishermen.

Divers flock to the Berry Islands for such delights as the underwater rock formations near Chub Cay and big staghorn coral reefs. Also an as yet unidentified wreck with cannons can be seen.

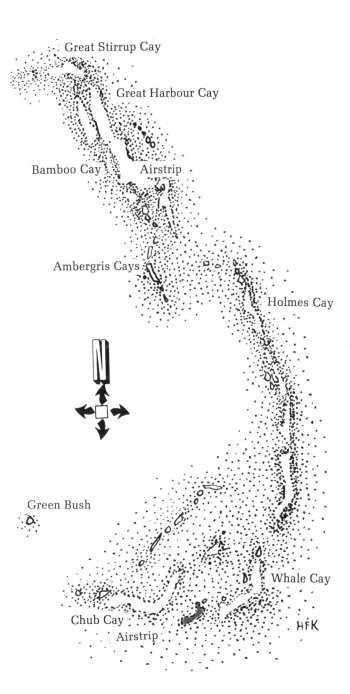

BIMINI and CAT CAY

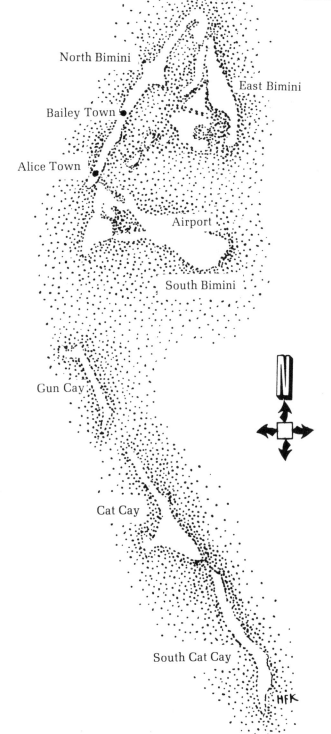

North Bimini

East Bimini

Bailey Town

Alice Town

Airport

South Bimini

Gun Cay

Cat Cay

South Cat Cay

HFK

Because it is only fifty miles east of Miami and because nearby waters offer some of the best fishing in the Bahamas – which is to say, the world – Bimini and its neighboring islets beside the Gulf Stream are world-famous for sports fishing. The marlin catches are known all over the fishing fraternity's range. The air and boat service to the mainland is excellent. Excellent, too, are the accommodations at Alice Town, the resort center.

The three settlements on the small islands are Alice Town, Bailey Town, and Porgy Bay. Nightlife is delightful and informal, and there are a number of good and well-known hotels here. The Big Game Fishing Club is the shrine of game fishermen. Bimini is where the late inventor George "Bert" Lyon built a million-dollar estate at Paradise Point and took up water skiing at the age of sixty-one. He also roller-skated in his patio.

South of Bimini is Cat Cay. Privately owned, it is a paradise for the members of Cat Cay Club with a fine golf course, a big Marina, beautiful white sand beaches, swimming pool, landing for seaplanes, many private homes in secluded settings, and, of course, club facilities, clubhouse, restaurants and bars.

INAGUA

Second largest of the Bahamas, this vast southern windward island is home to about 900 people and twenty-eight thousand flamingoes. Naturalists are enchanted with its beauty and its mystery, and its magnificent birds, which also include roseate spoonbills, herons, egrets, and hummingbirds. Bats live in inland caves. Wild horses, donkeys, cattle, and hogs roam the island. The flamingoes that once graced all the Bahamas now make their last retreat in Windsor Lake on Great Inagua. Though they home there by the thousands, they are very wary of approaching man and it is difficult to photograph them in all their multitudinous beauty. However, this can be done if the photographer crawls through the surrounding swamp on his stomach, for they do not scout the landscape at a level lower than their shoulders.

Mathew Town is thriving today, largely because of West India Chemicals Company, in which the Morton Salt Company has a controlling interest. The salt is produced in huge salinas at the rate of about a quarter of a million tons a year. The company has built roads, an electrical plant, a well-equipped hospital, and even a moving-picture theater. Inagua is surrounded by a reef and has no good harbors. The tourists who will learn to love this enchanting island are still waiting in the wings.

There is a legend that there is a great cache of gold hidden on the northern end of

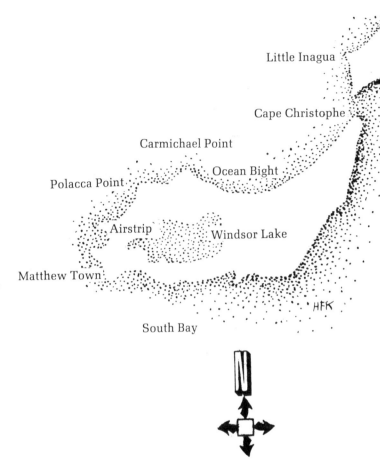

Inagua by the Haitian tyrant Henri Cristophe, who is said to have built a summer palace here. Inagua is nearer Haiti than are any other Bahama islands. South of Inagua in 1687 Captain Phipps brought up twenty-six tons of Spanish treasure.

ACKLINS, CROOKED, FORTUNE AND CASTLE ISLANDS

This group of four islands and their cays form a ring around the large lagoon known as Acklins Bight, once rich in sponges before they were killed by a fungoid. Though they are administered as the Crooked Island District, they are usually known collectively as Long Cay. Columbus came here looking for gold and sailed off down the Crooked Island Passage, the seaway for large ships steaming toward South America. Because these islands were once notorious as the retreat of pirates who attacked ships in the nearby Passage, the ancient rusty cannon near the beach at French Wells on Crooked Island is thought to be a remainder of a pirate fortification.

On the northern cliff of Crooked Island the 112-foot Bird Rock Lighthouse guides the way to the entrance of the Passage. Here Portland offers shelter in any winds to vessels drawing up to ten feet. Not far south is the settlement of Landrail Point. Nearby a new real-estate development is being built. Crooked Island has an airstrip, and there are roads on Crooked and Acklins islands, but this part of the Bahamas is just at the dawn of its development. The landmark of Fortune Island is Fortune Hill, which can be seen twelve miles away. The small settlement of Albert Town was once a bustling community but is now almost a ghost town. Another lighthouse on tiny Castle Island marks the Caribbean end of the Crooked Island Passage. There is a dangerous sunken reef seven miles to the west, where many ancient wrecks have been reported.

GOVERNMENT

At precisely 12:01 a.m., on July 10, 1973 as thousands cheered in Nassau's Clifford Park, full nationhood for the Commonwealth of the Bahamas became a reality as the new Bahamas flag of black, aquarmarine and gold unfurled in the midnight air.

This brought to a close some 250 years of colonial rule, but it did not end monarchical ties as the Bahamas Government opted to remain in the Commonwealth of Nations with Her Majesty continuing as Head of State. Self-governing since 1964, the Bahamas took from the Crown on July 10 the three remaining areas which had been subject to the British Governor's jurisdiction – defense, internal security and external affairs. The new nation,

Independence Celebration, July 10, 1973. *The photograph shows from left to right (first row): Governor Sir John Paul, Prince Charles, Prime Minister and Mrs. Lynden O. Pindling and Governor-General Designate Sir Milo Butler.*

beginning August 1, 1973, had its first Bahamian Governor General, the Hon. Milo B. Butler, Sr., serving as the Queen's Representative. Following his death, Sir Gerald Cash became Governor-General.

The constitution includes provisions safeguarding the fundamental freedoms of the individual regardless of race, place of origin, political opinion, colour, creed or sex. These fundamental rights are subject to enforcement by the Supreme Court.

Parliament consists, as previously, of The Queen, the Senate and the House of Assembly. The Senate consists of 9 members appointed by the Governor General on the advice of the Prime Minister, and 4 members appointed by the Governor General on the advice of the Leader of the Opposition and three members appointed by the Governor on the advice of the Prime Minister after consultation with the Leader of the Opposition.

The House of Assembly consists of 43 members. In the general election of June 10, 1982, the government party won 32 of the 43 seats.

Parliament can be prorogued or dissolved by the Governor General on the advice of the Prime Minister, provided that if the Prime Minister has lost the support of the majority of members of the House of Assembly the Governor General will dissolve Parliament if no successor can otherwise be found. In any event Parliament will not continue for more than five years from the date of its first sitting after any dissolution. In times of war, however, Parliament may extend its life for a period not exceeding 12 months at a time but only up to a maximum of two years.

The Governor General appoints as Prime Minister the person from the House of Assembly who, in his judgement, is best able to command the support of the majority of the members of that House.

There is a Cabinet consisting of the Prime Minister and not less than eight other Ministers.

There is a Supreme Court consisting of the Chief Justice and such number of other Justices as may be prescribed by Parliament. There is also a Court of Appeal consisting of a President, the Chief Justice and such number of Justices of Appeal as may be prescribed by Parliament. Provision is made for appeals from the Court of Appeal to the Judicial Committee of Her Majesty's Privy Council, or to such other court as may be prescribed by Parliament.

Modern Bahamian history has had its share of dramatic changes. Prior to the granting of independence on July 10, perhaps the two most significant events occurred during January – the first on January 7, 1964 when the islands received internal self-government under a written constitution, and the second on January 10, 1967 when, for the first time, a majority party, led by Lynden O. Pindling, won the government.

Actually, both reforms began in 1956, for in that year the fledgling Progressive Liberal Party challenged the long-entrenched United Bahamian Party with sufficient strength to give the Bahamas a real two-party system. After a meeting of Bahamas representatives with British officials in the Colonial Of-

fice in London in 1963, a new constitution followed, patterned on the British parliamentary system.

The 43-member House of Assembly is the major legislative body and is elected by universal suffrage. Women received the vote in 1960. Each member of the House represents a specified district, though he does not have to live in it. Members of the House are elected for five-year terms.

Lynden O. Pindling, born in 1930 in Nassau, received his primary-school education there and studied law at the University of London. He came to the highest post in the government after many years in the House of Assembly as leader of the Progressive Liberal Party, long the official Party of the Opposition. He has achieved a reputation as an astute man of goodwill and diplomacy, intent on achieving peaceful prosperity for the people he represents. In the Queen's New Year's Honours, 1983, the Prime Minister was knighted and is now Sir Lynden Pindling, KCMG, MP.

Just prior to the Independence Celebrations in 1973, Prime Minister Pindling said:

"One might say that the Bahama Islands lost their sovereignty some 481 years ago when Christopher Columbus opened up the new world by landing on San Salvador. Since that time a number of attempts have been made to regain that sovereignty and, finally, on July 10, 1973, the Bahamian people will be able to realize the dreams and aspirations of all those before them who have sought nationhood for our 700 Islands.

"It will be a prideful time on July 10 when the new flag is raised high and the Constitutional Instruments denoting Independence are passed from the Crown to our hands. But what of July 11 and thereafter? I have said before that Independence of itself promises no bed of roses, but my Government will gladly assume the responsibility and continue to shoulder the burdens for the peace, order and progress of a sovereign Bahamas. All Bahamians, regardless of race, place of origin, political opinion, colour or creed, are invited to join in a massive national effort to help build this great land of ours."

As the third oldest parliamentary democracy in this hemisphere, following Bermuda and Barbados, the Bahamas holds a unique position in the western world, according to Prime Minister Pindling.

"In no other part of the hemisphere," he said, "do all the social, economic, political and security considerations merge into one focal spot as they do in the Bahamas, thereby making it a pivotal point in hemispheric relations."

In a speech accepting United Nations membership on September 19, 1973, Mr. Pindling said, "we believe that we can make a contribution to a better international understanding by sharing our experiences in human relations in effecting change without disorder, revolution without bloodshed and in developing a stable economic and social order."

AIRLINES AND AIRPORTS

The Bahamas have excellent scheduled daily airline service by international carriers and by local lines, which link the islands with the rest of the world, and Nassau and Grand Bahama with the Family Islands. Nassau International Airport and Freeport International Airport are the principal international ports of entry.

Frequent daily jet flights are scheduled between United States cities and Nassau and Freeport. British Air links Nassau to London, Bermuda and Jamaica. Air Canada schedules regular flights between Nassau and Montreal and Toronto.

There are 54 airports and airstrips in The Bahamas, variously owned and operated – some by The Bahamas government, some by private owners, and some by the U.S. Air Force. The islands with airports and airstrips are Abaco, Acklins Island, Andros, Berry Islands, Bimini, Cat Island, Cay Sal, Crooked Island, Eleuthera, Exumas, Grand Bahama Island, Inagua, Long Island, Mayaguana, New Providence, Ragged Island, Rum Cay and San Salvador.

PRIVATE FLYING

Island hopping among The Bahamas has become one of the favorite adventures of private-flying enthusiasts. Exploring this land and its beautiful water by air has been made easy by the plentiful supply of airports and airstrips.

All flight arrivals and departures into and from The Bahamas must be made through airports designated as ports of entry. Basic requirements for flying in the islands are radio equipment for two-way communication on all required frequencies, overwater survival gear for all occupants, aeronautical charts and, for Family Island flights, sturdy tiedown stakes and ropes. Fixed-base operators at airports of departure in Miami, Fort Lauderdale, and West Palm Beach are thoroughly familiar with all Customs and Immigration requirements for flights to and from The Bahamas, and will gladly assist in the preparation of all necessary documents; they will also rent or sell survival equipment for overwater flights.

On arrival at a port-of-entry airport in The Bahamas, visitors must first of all visit Customs and Immigration officials for proper clearance. United States citizens are not required to carry passports and visas, but they should have citizenship identification. Other nationals should carry passports. Bahamian Special Declarations must be filled out in triplicate to be surrendered to Customs and Immigration officers on arrival. These forms may be obtained from base operators at ports of departure or from officials at entry ports in The Bahamas. Because flights between the United States and the Bahamas penetrate the Atlantic Defense Identification Zone (ADIZ), DVFR flight plans must be filed and observed both ways. A departure tax of $5 per person will be paid for passengers, but not for the crew of the airplane.

For interisland travel, flight plans are required on all flights departing from Nassau, and are desirable on departures from other islands. Flight plans may be filed wherever there are radio facilities for communications with Nassau Air Traffic Control. IFR flight plans are required for all flights at night. In island-to-island travel, an extra copy of The Bahamian Special Declaration, which also functions as a cruising permit, should be carried and produced on the request of a commissioner or customs officer at any airport visited.

Radio and navigational facilities in The Bahama Islands are excellent, considering that this is an offshore island area. Five Omni Stations are now in operation in the Bahamas. They are situated at Bimini, at Freeport on Grand Bahama Island, Treasure Cay on the island of Abaco, Governor's Harbour on the island of Eleuthera and at Nassau. Homing beacons are located at many convenient places throughout the islands. Towers are in operation at Nassau International Airport, at Freeport and West End on Grand Bahama Island, and (for communication only) at the U.S. Air Force base at Gold Rock Creek, Grand Bahama. Unicom Stations are maintained at many resorts in the Family Islands. For communication with Air Traffic Control in Nassau, six peripheral radio stations have now been established in the Family Islands, stretching as far to the southeast as Great Inagua.

TOURISM

Tourism as an industry on which millions of people depend for their living is a phenomenon peculiar to the twentieth century, and it is tied in with some other twentieth-century developments. The great migration to the sun began some hundred years ago and is a by-product of improved transportation and communications. The first horde of sun seekers went west to Southern California, lured by the railroads' lyrical descriptions. The second great wave came to Florida in the 1920s, pouring down the Dixie Highway in Tin Lizzies to one of the dizziest land booms ever known. Bahama tourism is a product of the jet age. Fast and dependable aircraft have made island hopping practical and popular.

A great tourist economy requires more than sun, sand and sea, and good transportation. Tourism requires telling the world about it – publicity, promotion, advertising. Though some called it "utter folly," in 1950 the Bahamas Legislature decided to spend considerable money for the promotion of tourism. Bahamians observed that tourism in south Florida is a clean and attractive industry that is the principal means of support for more than a million people and that it molds attractive communities and offers many jobs. Therefore, to some extent they followed the south Florida promotion pattern in expending their money and energies.

First they courted wealthy vacationers in the northeastern United States and Canada in winter months: They lured some of the hordes of Miami Beach winter visitors over to take a look at the islands across the Gulf Stream. Then, as jets came in and fares came down and hotels were built, they started building a summer season. They expounded on the charms of low-cost vacations in what had been slack months, they boasted about the pleasant summer climate, too, and the summers became lively. They extended the promotion to Great Britain and Europe during the 1960s, with the extension of jet service, and the results have proved rewarding. Castro's takeover of Cuba diverted many vacationers who had previously visited that island to the Bahamas.

At first, during the 1960s, the many segments of the south Florida tourist industry, which centers upon Miami Beach, were uneasy, fearing the competition. The airlines and the hotels envisioned a large diversion of sun seekers from their old haunts. Soon, however, the south Florida tourist industry recognized that the Bahamas are an asset. Hotels have package plans that allow the visitor to stay a week on Miami Beach and a week in the Bahamas at special rates. Airlines promote package tours called "Floribbean," which include a trip to the Bahamas. The result is a mounting tide of vacationers of moderate means, the ones that make tourism a stable industry.

The islands have a major ingredient of the age-old dreams of men – serene, remote, and beautiful beaches gleaming in a world that is always balmy beside a blue sea. Now they have a way to get there and pleasant places to stay. The Bahamas Ministry of Tourism has done an inspired and skilled job in telling the world about it. The government has done as well in working with the developers of the new resorts. These are men who are inspired by an unusual and peculiar creative genius, as well as by hopes of making money. Some have all the money anyone could ever need and have been moved by the sense that they can build a new way of life. The ingredients needed to keep tourism booming indefinitely are all there, including the dozens of islands still waiting in the sun for their day to come.

FISHING AND FISH

Because the sports fishermen were the first outsiders to rediscover the Bahamas in the twentieth century, the islanders know how to welcome them and treat them well. The waters have the fish, the islanders have the charter boats and the expertise as guides. From the indigo waters of the Gulf Stream, where the marlin leap, to the shallow flats where bantam bonefish put up a mighty fight, the marine world offers a wonderful variety of fish.

The blue marlin is awe inspiring when hooked. The record Bahamas marlin for 130-pound line is 742 pounds; the fish was caught off Bimini. For a long time most fishermen thought that the eastern edge of the Gulf Stream off Bimini, Cat Cay, Grand Bahama, and Walker Cay was the only area in the Bahama waters in which the fighting blues abound. Now they have been caught in the Tongue of the Ocean off Andros Town, within the Northwest Channel beside Chub Cay in the Berry Islands, off Abaco and near Harbour Island, and off the coasts of the lower sides of Eleuthera. In beauty and fight, the big blue marlin is the ace of all game fish. It takes know-how and the right rigs to hook them, strength and skill to boat them. They are caught throughout the Bahamas, and the peak season is from June through August.

King of the fall and winter migratory visitors is the wahoo, a fish that packs a striking wallop. The wahoo's speed requires skill in fishing and in boat handling. Top wahoo grounds are in the Tongue of the Ocean, the Northeast and Northwest Providence channels near Nassau, and Exuma Sound around Powell's Point in Eleuthera. The Bahamas' record wahoo weighed 149 pounds and was caught off Cat Cay in June 1962.

Another big fellow is the bluefin tuna, tackle buster of the western Bahamas. This fish, the giant of the mackerel family, weighs up to a thousand pounds. Schools of tuna flow across the western Bahamas Banks in May and early June. They are also found in deep waters throughout the summer.

Many expert anglers prefer stalking bonefish to fighting the big ones in the blue water. They consider it the most challenging form of the sport. The bonefish is a wary fighter, which roots up crabs from the bottom of shallow flats. His tail breaks water as he feeds, and that is the signal for the stalking fisherman to cast just so in front of the feeding fish. The fight that the bonefish puts up is a delight to light-tackle fishermen. Bonefish are plentiful throughout the islands' shallows all the year round.

There are hosts of other thrilling catches. The Allison yellowfin tuna is found in all deepwater areas of the Bahamas during June, July, and August and occasionally in other months. The amberjack is a fighting fish that may be hooked from November through May in reefy areas. Blackfin tuna are very plentiful around Nassau from May through September and are found in all deepwater areas. Bonito are summer visitors, May through September, in deepwater areas and are plentiful around Nassau. The beautiful dolphin are hooked in deep water in winter and spring. Kingfish school during the winter all over the Bahama waters and are also plentiful in May, June, and July. Tail-walking sailfish are hooked in the fall, winter, and spring around Berry Islands, Bimini, Cat Cay, Grand Bahama, Walker Cay, and Exuma Sound. The grouper is the good old stay-at-home, found year round in reefy spots throughout the islands.

The Bahamas offer excellent sport on all types of tackle. The big ones are in the blue water. Many of the meat-on-table fish in the green waters of the coral reefs around the countless islands can put up a good battle. Many of them take a trolled lure, and they will all snatch a live bait. Fishing was never better than in the bays, passes, inlets, and creeks of the Bahamas. Here there is fast and consistently steady action for the fly fisherman, plug caster, and spinning enthusiast. Several species of snapper and grouper lie close to the bottom and take weighted lures. Fishing clubs, hotels, and inns abound in the major islands and are found on many of the smaller cays. Headquarters for charter boatmen are Bimini, Nassau, Grand Bahama, Eleuthera, Abaco, Andros, Chub Cay, and Walker Cay. There are hundreds of genial native guides who will show newcomers where and how to hook them.

SAILING IN THE BAHAMAS

The ideal way to see the Bahamas is by sea, and the ideal craft for the purpose is a motor sailer, according to yachtsmen. The trade winds are usually steady, from the east and southeast, and so it is good to have power to proceed to windward when heading from Florida. Shallow-draft yachts drawing less than six feet are best, while a centerboarder such as the islanders build is best of all. A yacht drawing three to four feet can go just about anywhere. Yachts drawing as much as nine feet have made successful cruises in the Bahamas.

The U.S. Hydrographic Office has published small-scale chart series H.O. 5990-5995, made from aerial surveys, and these are the most accurate charts to date. Lighthouses and beacons in the islands are maintained by the government of the Bahamas.

Nassau is one of the great yachting capitals of the world, and has everything the cruising yachtsman needs, but there are also many fine marinas and wonderful yacht clubs throughout the islands. Many good and experienced guides are to be found, men who know the waters and have taken cruises throughout the Bahamas.

Yachts should enter Bahamian waters through a port of entry, of which there are 38 for boats throughout the islands. A yellow quarantine flag should be flown and no contact made with the shore other than tying up until the boarding officer has come aboard. An International Maritime Declaration of Health, in lieu of a Bill of Health, is accepted from arriving yachts.

In recent years a number of radio aides have added safety to cruising in these waters. Radio Station ZNS at Nassau, 1540 on the dial, is on the air twenty-four hours a day with occasional weather reports. The station also makes personal-message broadcasts, and the service is available to everyone.

Three sailing routes are the favored tracks of yachts from Florida to Nassau. One of them proceeds from Palm Beach to Freeport or West End, Grand Bahama Island, fifty-five miles across the Gulf Stream. It passes to the eastward across the Little Bahama Bank, around Great Abaco Island, down to Eleuthera Island, and from there to Nassau. A second favored course from Miami or Port Everglades proceeds up and around Great Isaac Light, then to and around Great Stirrup Cay in the Berry Islands, and down to Nassau. This is the sailing route over which the annual Miami-Nassau Ocean Yacht Race is sailed, and it is also the deepwater route for vessels of any draft.

A third popular route from Miami to Nassau is to Gun Cay, over the Great Bahama Bank to Northwest Channel Light, and thence to Nassau. On this route the ship can go into Bimini, Gun Cay, Cat Cay, with their good harbors, or Chub Cay or Little Whale Cay in the Berry Islands.

Among the most popular of the Family Islands is beautiful Eleuthera, which has good harbors, excellent marinas, and splendid yacht clubs from one end of the island to the other. Spanish Wells, a quaint and attractive little seafaring village, and Harbour Island, which has one of the best harbors in the Bahamas, lie just off the northern end of Eleuthera. Rock Sound, on the southwestern coast, has a good harbor, an excellent marina, and a superlative yacht club. Hatchet Bay's fine landlocked harbor is used as a hurricane refuge by boats of the islands.

Mysterious Andros is well worth a visit. It has one harbor, Middle Bight, which will take deep-draft vessels. Andros Town on Fresh Creek is a very elegant resort village. The Exuma Cays offer miles and miles of cruising among a string of beautiful little islands, which provide many good anchorages and some very good harbors. The best is at Allen Cay, a safe harbor in all winds that can take vessels up to ten feet in draft. No yachtsman should miss the Out Island Regatta, held annually at George Town on Great Exuma Island in the spring of the year. Here the Family Islanders compete in sailing craft they have built themselves, and spectator yachts come from all over the Western Hemisphere. Ashore the Family Islanders and their guests celebrate the event in a sort of marine version of Mardi Gras. George Town is a quaint and attractive village, with five miles of fine beaches and marinas.

UNDERWATER RESEARCH AND TREASURE HUNTING

One fascinating aspect of the Bahamas is that they are involved in the exploration of the last two great frontiers on which men stand today, outer space and the ocean's depths. Tracking stations on the islands provide beacons for astronauts in orbit. In the clear waters surrounding the islands, major research is going on concerning the undersea world.

Pioneers such as Jon Lindbergh and Robert Stenuit made some of the first studies in Bahama waters on how to live under the sea. They descended 430 feet into waters off Great Stirrup Cay in the Berry Islands in a SPID (Submersible Portable Inflatable Dwelling). There they lived under great pressure for two days and nights in an underwater capsule called *Sea Diver.* Their initial experiments have led to further experiments.

Edward Link, who built the *Sea Diver,* is one of the pioneers in underwater exploration and has done work in the Bahamas for years. The inventor of the Link air trainer for training aircraft pilots, he turned his inventive genius from the sky to the sea. He is developing other deepwater vessels capable of exploring great depths. Treasure hunting in the waters that were once pirate-infested is one of Mr. Link's hobbies, and he has invented very sophisticated devices useful to both underwater archeologists and to treasure hunters.

Dr. Jacques Piccard, a distinguished second-generation undersea pioneer, has also gathered information from Bahama waters. He is the inventor of the mesoscaphe, a medium-depth submarine. He also specializes in undersea acoustics and communications.

The Aluminaut, the deep-diving submarine of Reynolds International, Inc., has brought up from the great depths off the Bahamas chunks of rocks that have turned out to be 40 per cent manganese and 24 per cent phosphate. Reynolds found a thousand square miles of manganese lying on the bottom of the sea, and there is evidence of other minerals. The United States now imports ninety per cent of its manganese, which is used in hardening steel.

The waters of the Bahamas are clear because the islands have no rivers to carry sediment to sea. They are also unpolluted and tropically warm, which makes them ideal for research and undersea developments. The same qualities make them great for treasure hunting. It is well known that there is still Spanish and pirate treasure there, waiting to be found, for the evidence turns up from time to time. By law, treasure hunters must be licensed and wrecks registered. In the islands, old gold coins have been uncovered on beaches, and wrecks of the Spanish plate fleets have been found in the sea. Buried pirate gold has been unearthed on land. In assessing tales of treasure, one should remember that these waters

and the hundreds of cays were once the homeland of the pirate fleet that raided Spanish shipping carrying gold, silver and emeralds from Peru and Mexico home to Spain. They usually sailed from Havana up the Gulf Stream along the Florida Coast before turning east to home. In addition to the plundering pirates, there are also records in Spanish archives of numerous Spanish fleets being cast ashore and wrecked by hurricanes in the seventeenth and eighteenth centuries.

As far back as 1687 (as mentioned earlier in this book), treasure hunters were bringing up vast wealth from the depths around the Bahama Islands; Captain John Smith retrieved twenty-six tons of gold from the wreck of a Spanish galleon near Turks Island in that year. Fortune Island, in the Long Cay group in the southern Bahamas, is said to be the site of a buried pirate treasure. Probably one of the most promising areas for treasure hunters lies west of Acklins and Castle islands in the southern Bahamas. There, ocean-going vessels pass through Crooked Island Passage, the route to the Caribbean. Seven miles west of tiny Castle Island at the tip of Acklins Island, and on the western edge of the Passage, is a very dangerous reef with scattered coral heads. The Spaniards named these islets, very properly, Mira Por Vos ("Look Out for Yourself"). An untold number of ancient wrecks have been littered on this reef, and even the wreckers have given these dangerous waters a wide berth.

What the treasure hunter looks for first is ballast rocks, smooth river-worn stones that were carried in old sailing ships to stabilize them. They are good clues, because they obviously are not of marine origin. Skilled underwater explorers are also attracted by straight lines or geometric curves, which are evidence of something manmade; artists, with an eye for this sort of thing, have proved to be skilled in spotting sunken finds of things made by man, whether they be wrecks of ships or articles of archeological interest. For decades, treasure hunters have been working on electronic devices that could detect metal underwater. A group of Florida treasure hunters in the 1930s developed just such an instrument to find sunken treasure in the waters bordering the Gulf Stream. Their instrument didn't work well over water, and they sold it to the United States government as the mine detector of World War II. Since that time, much more sophisticated and successful devices have been developed.

GOLF IN THE BAHAMAS

There are about 16 golf courses floating in a turquoise ocean. Some are easy, some are hard. Some are for casual keeping in shape, some are for taxing every nerve and muscle in your body.

The courses are well-maintained. Plenty of golf carts if you want them. Enough courses so you don't spend a lot of time waiting to get on. There are golf pros to help take the kinks out of your swing, if you like, or to help you get up a foursome if that's all you need.

NASSAU

Blue Hill Golf Club and Golf Range – This course is sheltered by the Blue Hills of southern New Providence Island. It is a 1,286-yard, par-3, 9-hole course. And it is the only course on the island with illuminated driving range, putting green, miniature course and chipping greens for night play. Designed by C.C. Shaw, the course is popular with both amateurs and experts, for it has a minimum of two bunkers at each hole and many man-made lakes.

Coral Harbour Golf Club – Designed by golf pro and architect George Fazio, this course is one of the most challenging in the Western Hemisphere. There are wooded roughs, rolling fairways, numerous water hazards and treacherous bunkers. Rivalling any other for beauty, outclassing most in toughness, the 18-hole championship, 6,710-yard, par-70 course also is one of the most interesting you will find.

Paradise Island Golf Club – This course is an 18-hole, 6,966-yard, par-72 championship course situated on the eastern end of famous

Paradise Island resort. The turquoise waters of the Atlantic are on the north, the placid green waters of Montagu Bay are on the south. The links feature thick brush-bordered, rolling fairways, several doglegs and numerous bunkers, deep lakes and tightly trapped, elevated greens.

Ambassador Beach Golf Club – One of the newest courses in Nassau lies adjacent to one of the newest hotels on the island of New Providence. The 18-hole, 6,800-yard, par-72 championship course is open to visitors as well as members and guests. The first tee and clubhouse are only two minutes away from any guest room. To make the course a challenging one, 13 lakes have been added to the existing terrain.

South Ocean Golf Club – This is the newest course on New Providence Island. It is located at the southwestern end of the island, and the high ground gives you a panoramic view of the Tongue of the Ocean. Designed by Joe Lee, this course is an 18-hole, 6,707-yard, par-72 championship one. There are four water holes, two on the front nine and two on the back nine.

GRAND BAHAMA

Bahama Reef Golf and Country Club – You will find that this championship 18-hole, par-72 course is a challenge to every golfer. It is 1,000 feet from the ocean, adjacent to the beach resort area and within walking distance of five hotels.

Fourtune Hills Golf and Country Club – One of the most spectacular courses on Grand Bahama. This Championship 18-hole course rambles over 150 acres of high Lucayan terrain. There are forests, insidious traps, bunkers and man-made lakes.

Grand Bahama Country Club, Westend – Challenging is the name of the game at this big and sprawling self-contained resort. The 18-hole, 6,800 yard, championship par-72 course sets the pace for Grand Bahama's reputation as the place to go for golf. There are excellent fairways and greens over rolling terrain, seven man-made and natural lakes, and seventy well-placed bunkers and a cultivated rough. An additional 9 holes feature seven new water hazards and offers an alternate pattern to your play. They extend the course to 10,450 yards.

Bahamas Princess Golf Club – Here is one of the world's finest golf resorts, imaginatively and cleverly thought out to challenge any level of golfer. Duplicated here are the most interesting holes of the best Dick Wilson courses. This is a new approach to golf resort design – a golf control centre containing 250 golf carts connecting directly to the hotel lobby. The fairways are well-trapped; the greens are well-isolated; there are five man-made lakes adding to the challenge. Near this course lies the "Princess Ruby," a second 18-hole championship layout.

Lucayan Golf and Country Club – This course, designed by Dick Wilson, is one of the richest and greenest ones in the world. It sits on a naturally hilly area overlooking picturesque Bell Channel. Although there is only one lake on the 6,859-yard links, Lucayan offers a great challenge, especially when the golfer strays from the fairway into the tough rough. The wind is an important factor here, too. The course was the site of the 1971 B$130,000 Bahamas International Open Championship.

Shannon Golf and Country Club – This is one of the newer courses in Freeport/Lucaya and the site of the Grand Bahama International Golf Tournament. Designed by Joe Lee, the 6,810-yard course has wide, roomy fairways bounded by jungle-like foliage. There are many challenging holes to be found. The 210-yard, par-three 13th and the 525-yard 10th both include play around and over water.

ELEUTHERA

Cape Eleuthera Golf Club – Emerging as one of the most spectacular courses in the Bahamas, this course has been designed by architects Bruce Devlin and Bob von Hagge. It has been carved out of acre after acre of rolling terrain at the southern tip of this 100-mile-long island. The course is built along the edge of the Atlantic.

Cotton Bay – This course is the product of master golf architect Robert Trent Jones. It is a layout of breathtaking beauty with some greens perched on promontories overlooking the Atlantic breakers below. With 127 traps and strong winds, this rolling seaside course is a rugged one. Throughout, it has a series of dogleg holes.

BERRY ISLANDS

Great Harbour Club – This 18-hole championship course, designed by the noted golf architect, Joe Lee, is said to be one of the top ten golf courses in the world. A par-72, it measures 6,565 yards from the men's tees and 7,010 from the championship tees. The first hole, just steps away from the beautiful clubhouse, is some 70 feet above the sea, and the view is spectacular.

ABACO

Treasure Cay Golf Club – Dick Wilson-designed, this Golf Club is built around what is to become a complete residential area. It brings the world of golf right to the doorsteps of guests and residents of this pictureque oceanside resort. High-rolling fairways are border-spotted with tropical brush. Sharp-rising, broad greens are cleverly guarded by nearby lakes and deep sand traps, two characteristic features of a Wilson-built course. In this 7,012 yards of natural landscape, it is difficult to choose one hole over another. Across this championship 18-hole, par-72 course, there is always a gentle onshore breeze.

TRADE AND COMMERCE

Nassau is the financial as well as the political center of the islands, but Freeport has become the industrial center. This is due largely to the unique taxation freedoms granted to the area under the Hawksbill Creek Act. Among the other islands, the government's Industries Encouragement Act is also proving effective in stimulating light industries for export. Thus, though tourism is certainly the most important element in correcting the age-old imbalance of trade, other significant new projects are helping to stabilize the economy.

The major exports of the islands today are pulpwood, cement, salt, cinematographic films, rum, crawfish, and vegetables. Real exports are only about one tenth of the value of imports. New and exciting projects are under way. It was long believed that the islands had no mineral resources. Recent geological surveys by petroleum companies have afforded some indication that oil may be found in the fossil coral and limestone beneath the surface, for such formations have proved to be oil "traps" in other areas of the world. The Petroleum Act provides for oil exploration, prospecting, and mining under licenses.

The Family Islands are also beginning to enjoy their share of the new industrial and commercial development. Woven articles of straw — palmetto and sisal — and shell work are the traditional native handicrafts. Much is sold to tourists but some is exported. Pulpwood, sugar, canned tomatoes, and salt are among the major exports. Frozen crawfish, the so-called "Florida lobster," is another major export. Pineapple, canned as fruit and juice, is produced in considerable quantity. Bacardi rum interests have recently built one of the largest and most modern rum distilleries in the world near Nassau, at Coral Harbour on New Providence Island.

The most exciting frontier of development in the Bahamas may prove to be not the building of superlative resorts but the commercial exploration of the undersea world around the islands. Movie makers, such as Ivan Tors with his "Flipper" motion pictures and TV series, have discovered that the clarity and warmth of the water and the beauty of the coral reefs are ideal for underwater filming. The porpoise Flipper commited regularly from the Miami Seaquarium to the Bahamas for much of his undersea work. These and similar films such as the James Bond *Thunderball*, filmed off Nassau, are responsible for the fact that "cinematographic films" are an appreciable item among the Bahamas exports.

TAXES AND INVESTMENT

It is not by accident that Nassau has become the Switzerland of the Western World, an international financial center. The tax structure and the laws regulating banking have been devised to court investors as hospitably as the islands court tourists. The Bahamas have no taxes on income, profits, capital gains, or accumulated profits; no dividend withholding tax, no taxes on franchises or share transfers, no inheritance taxes. The Bahamas government has no tax treaties with other nations.

The government obtains revenues for its functions from customs duties, licenses, payments by gambling casinos, passenger ticket and departure taxes, real-property taxes, a percentage of fire-insurance premiums, and a few other minor sources of internal revenue. Revenues are also obtained from licenses to airlines to operate scheduled flights.

Because of this tax structure, Bahama banks hold investors' funds from all over the world. About a dozen international banks, such as the Chase Manhattan Bank, operate there. There are even more investment banks, plus numerous trust companies affiliated with large banks, mutual fund companies, savings and loan associations, brokers, and finance companies.

There are several advantages to banking in Nassau's commercial banks. Deposits can be made in any freely convertible currency. The Bahamas government is stable. Accounts are confidential. Interest rates on time deposits are highly competitive and good. Heirs of persons with deposits in the Bahamas pay no Bahamian death, estate, or inheritance taxes.

Nassau's mutual funds have shown phenomenal growth in this decade. They also attract investors for a variety of reasons. Levering or gearing is not restricted in the Bahamas as it is in the United States. This means that shareholders in such funds can borrow up to the amount of their initial investment for the purchase of additional shares – which is fine, of course, on a rising market. Mutual fund accounts are confidential because the mutual fund companies are not required by law to divulge names of investors in their annual reports to the Bahamian government.

Most of the mutual funds managed in the Bahamas hold United States securities. Shareholders who are not citizens or residents of the United States may thus be freed from the United States estate or death tax normally imposed on those who invest directly in the United States. Investors in these mutual funds are free from capital gains taxes if the investment is not sold while the shareholder is actually in the United States, if he does not spend more than 183 days of the taxable year in the United States, and if he does not engage in any business or profession in the United States in that year.

Trust companies in the Bahamas manage assets from all over the world, especially from countries where conditions are unsettled or taxes and death duties are high. There is no problem in brokers' communications, since there is a direct telephone service to New York, Toronto, and London. It is due in considerable measure to the role played by these trust companies that the Bahamas have become an international finance center. They offer a full range of management services for Bahamian and foreign companies, and they are staffed by competent and knowlegeable personnel trained in other major banking centers of the world.

Many companies are chartered in the Bahamas in order to minimize taxes, and forming a company there is comparatively easy. Under the law of the islands there must be at least five shareholders.

Merchant bankers of Nassau today are channeling millions from investors for loans to governments and corporations in undeveloped countries. The banks issue bonds, notes, or debentures and sell them to investors.

There is a Post Office Savings Bank in Nassau with branches on eighteen other islands. Under the Banks and Trust Companies Regulation Act of 1965, it is required that any person transacting banking business in the Bahamas have a valid license issued by the governor.

The unit of monetary system is the Bahamian Dollar, same value as the U.S. Dollar. There is since 1974 a Central Bank of the Bahamas, with the mission to maintain the stability of exchange rates and regulate interest rates and the availability of credit in all its forms. Its functions include the issuance of currency and administration of exchange control. It serves as the government's banker and fiscal advisor and regulates the banking industry.

ENVOI

This, then is the Bahamas today: a world for both sun seekers and twentieth-century pioneers. The islands are a showplace of the Western World and its political and economic system. Here men and women are demonstrating that black and white can live and work together and in their cooperation accomplish great things. Here men and women are demonstrating what sort of world can be built when government and private enterprise cooperate to a high degree. The population is laced with three strains – from Great Britain, from Africa, and from the United States – and is founded on a common heritage of Anglo-Saxon legal and political institutions. Negros number about eighty-five percent of the population. This Negro majority today is proving that it can govern in fair, competent, and progressive fashion.

The thrust of government is to preserve the best of both worlds – the light-hearted and independent stance of the past and the promise of a creative and prosperous future. The Progressive Liberal Party is proving true to its name and its promises, by furthering a vigorous program of social and educational development, while at the same time following a course that encourages foreign investment, expanding tourism, and the diversification of the economy.

In the words of a former governor, Sir Ralph Grey, "All who live and work here depend on the interest and confidence of the world outside. We have good reason to be sure that if the world outside knows the facts about us, we shall have that interest and confidence."

With all the progress that has taken place, the islands still have much of what caused Columbus to write, "This country excels all others as far as the day surpasses the night in splendor." And the waters are still as he found them: "The sea is so transparent, we could see it to the bottom. The tropical fish rivaled the beauty of the flowers."

With all the diverse improvements that the last half of the twentieth century is bringing to the Bahamas, the islands still retain the enchantment of another, leisurely world. The past is ever-present, in the form of handsome old colonial mansions, quaint old villages that hug safe harbors, and thick stone fortresses. For those who have learned to love this beautiful world because it is remote and serene, there will be for ages plenty of lovely hideaways, small and private havens surround ed by the royal-blue ocean and the emerald shoals of the vast banks. There is much beauty still to be discovered in the world of the Bahamas, almost as much as when Columbus stepped ashore.

CONTENTS

Acknowledgements

In presenting herewith a completely revised edition of this popular volume on the Bahamas, I had the valuable assistance of William H. Kalis, Editor-in-Chief of the Bahamas News Bureau in Nassau, who checked every detail, to bring this book up to date. My special appreciation goes to him.

Richard Newstadt and Angela Briggs, both of the Bahamas Tourist Office in Miami, assisted me with many details in preparing this revised edition. My son, Michael Hannau, travelled with me to the islands, to photograph some new views for this book.

I will not forget those who assisted me for previous editions: Fred Maura, Keva Hanna Lawrence, the late Don McCarthy, and Roland Rose. I am grateful to all who contributed to this book.

May 1983   Hans W. Hannau

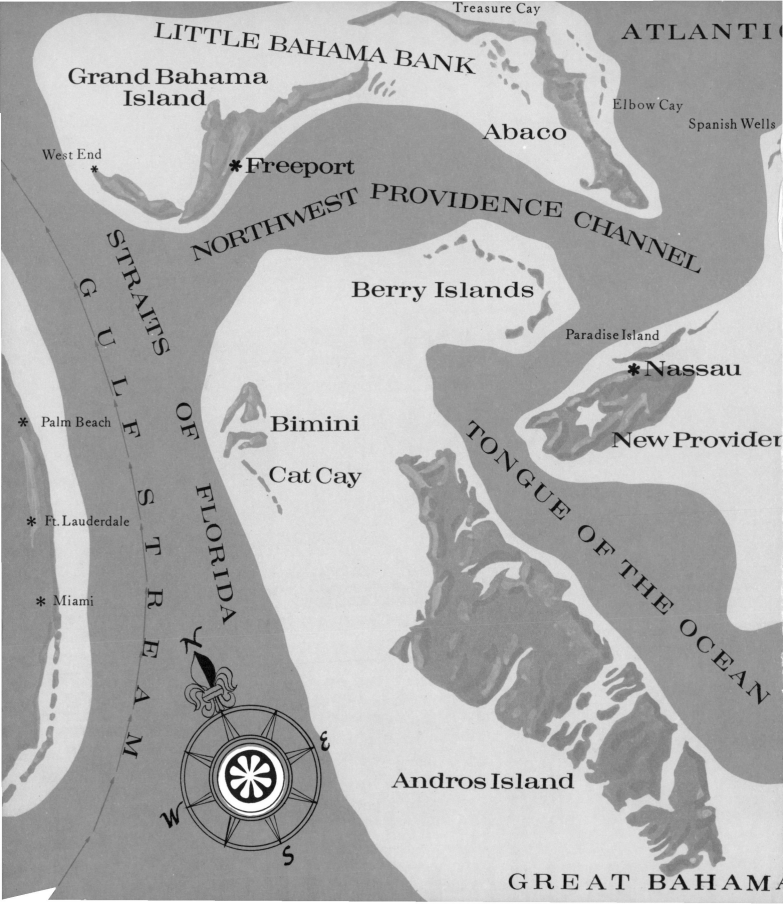